COLDITZ

To all Prisoners of War!

The escape from prison camps is no longer a sport!

Germany has always kept to the Hague Convention and only punished recaptured prisoners of war with minor disciplinary punishment.

Germany will still maintain these principles of international law.

But England has besides fighting at the front in an honest manner instituted an illegal warfare in non combat zones in the form of gangster commandos, terror bandits and sabotage troops even up to the frontiers of Germany.

They say in a captured secret and confidential English military pamphlet,

THE HANDBOOK OF MODERN IRREGULAR WARFARE:

". . . the days when we could practise the rules of sportsmanship are over. For the time being, every soldier must be a potential gangster and must be prepared to adopt their methods whenever necessary."

"The sphere of operations should always include the enemy's own country, any occupied territory, and in certain circumstances, such neutral countries as he is using as a source of supply."

England has with these instructions opened up a non military form of gangster war!

Germany is determined to safeguard her homeland, and especially her war industry and provisional centres for the fighting fronts. Therefore it has become necessary to create strictly forbidden zones, called death zones, in which all unauthorised trespassers will be immediately shot on sight.

Escaping prisoners of war, entering such death zones, will certainly lose their lives. They are therefore in constant danger of being mistaken for enemy agents or sabotage groups.

Urgent warning is given against making future escapes!

In plain English: Stay in the camp where you will be safe! Breaking out of it is now a damned dangerous act.

The chances of preserving your life are almost nil!

All police and military guards have been given the most strict orders to shoot on sight all suspected persons.

Escaping from prison camps has ceased to be a sport!

COLDITZ

THE GREAT ESCAPES

Ron Baybutt

LITTLE, BROWN AND COMPANY   BOSTON · TORONTO

CONTENTS

INTRODUCTION

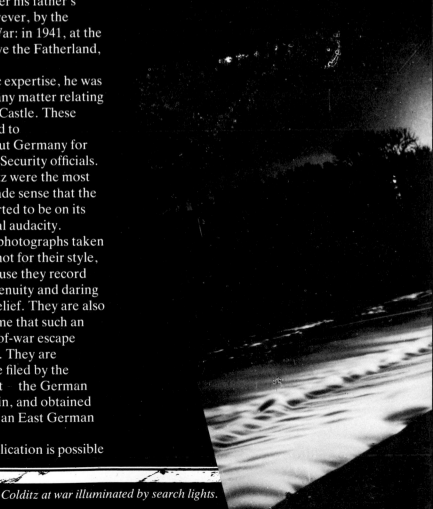

THE PHOTOGRAPHS that appear in this book were taken between the years 1941 and 1944 by Johannes Lange, who was born on 11 August, 1901, in the town of Colditz, which is situated twenty-two miles south-east of Leipzig in the district of Saxony, now part of the German Democratic Republic.

He was the only son of Moritz Lange, a lower middle-class professional man who added to his modest income as a photographer of christenings, weddings and sundry celebrations. It was a career that Johannes was to pursue under his father's tutelage. It was interrupted, however, by the outbreak of the Second World War: in 1941, at the age of forty, he was called to serve the Fatherland, but not as a soldier.

Because of his photographic expertise, he was ordered to take photographs of any matter relating to escape attempts from Colditz Castle. These photographs were then circulated to prisoner-of-war camps throughout Germany for the guidance and information of Security officials. The escape attempts from Colditz were the most ingenious, the most daring; it made sense that the rest of the country should be alerted to be on its guard against enterprises of equal audacity.

It is for this reason that the photographs taken by Johannes Lange are unique; not for their style, quality or composition, but because they record evidence of escape plots, the ingenuity and daring of which might otherwise defy belief. They are also unique because this is the first time that such an extensive collection of prisoner-of-war escape photographs has been published. They are prints from negatives which were filed by the Oberkommando der Wehrmacht — the German Army High Command – in Berlin, and obtained some thirty-five years later from an East German communist party official.

A sad irony is that their publication is possible only because the vast majority of the escape attempts were unsuccessful; obviously if they had been successful the photographs could not have been taken. It is not possible to state the total number of photographs taken by Lange. What is certain is that he made a handsome profit out of his privileged access to the Castle. In return for Red Cross food and cigarettes, he and his father took individual and group photographs which were sent to families and loved ones as proof of survival and good health. Some of these photographs also

Colditz at war illuminated by search lights.

A portrait of Johannes Lange taken by his father, Moritz.

appear in this book.

Lange, who processed his film in the first-floor flat of a large detached house in Fürstenweg, now renamed Karl Marx Ring, sold the food and cigarettes – apart from tinned sardines, which were his favourite fish – to the townspeople. The profits were such that after the war he was able to establish his own photographic business premises.

He died, a bachelor, on 22 April, 1975, leaving a small fortune of 109,000 East German Marks (£19,464) which, because he died intestate, was claimed by the state. He also left a remarkable legacy of historic photographs which vividly illustrate the invention, daring and stark courage of the prisoners-of-war in Colditz Castle.

THE HISTORY OF

THE STORY OF Colditz Castle spans almost a thousand years, and throughout that time its history has been mostly one of wars, violence and brutality. With its high, grey granite walls, barred windows, steep roofs, ancient towers, archways and moat, it would slip effortlessly into the pages of Bram Stoker's tales of Dracula.

Due to the ravages of war and time, it has been rebuilt and extended until it now totally dominates the town of Colditz which straddles the river Mulde in Saxony.

It was built originally in 1014 as a huge and resplendent royal hunting lodge for the kings of Saxony. Even in its early days it witnessed many a siege and battle, and during the Hussite wars of the fifteenth century it was almost completely destroyed. It was later rebuilt and given as a wedding present to a Danish princess on her marriage in 1583 to the Kurfuerst of Saxony.

During the Thirty Years War it came under heavy siege and in 1634 the town, allied to the Protestants, was sacked by the Imperialists. Swedish troops later recaptured the Castle and occupied it for several years. In 1706, during the war against Russia, the Swedes once again occupied the Castle. In more peaceful times, it was an official residence of the dukes of Saxony.

It was established as a prison in 1800. In 1828

its dungeons and bare comfortless rooms were used to subdue the insane. It became a prisoner-of-war camp after the German armies stormed through Poland in October 1939, and its Polish officer prisoners were joined by Belgian officers a year later.

The Oberkommando der Wehrmacht – the German Army High Command – in Berlin decided that the austere, unyielding Castle should be used as a *Sonderlager*; a special camp with maximum security to contain habitual escapers. It was later visited by Reichsmarschall Hermann Goering who declared Colditz to be escape-proof.

Theoretically, it made sense to contain persistent escapers under one roof. But, in practice, the success of the plan depended on two factors: the first was that it would indeed be impossible to escape, which, despite Goering's confident proclamation, wasn't quite the case; the second was the misplaced belief that the most inveterate escaper, faced with such tight security, would concede defeat once so incarcerated. That wasn't quite the case, either.

In fact, the Castle presented the kind of challenge that many of the British, French, Dutch, Polish and Belgian officers took as their duty to accept – and overcome. Furthermore, the German High Command had kindly assembled an

A deceptively pastoral scene, Colditz between the wars.

SCHLOSS COLDITZ

international array of talent that boasted an expert in almost every field from mechanical engineering to lock-picking and the manufacture of home-made explosives. While the sheer vastness of the place, with its sprawling attics, disused cellars and innumerable empty rooms, provided the facility to work secretly on such astonishing escape plans as the construction of a glider, which certainly wouldn't have been possible in a more conventional prisoner-of-war camp.

The number of prisoners caught attempting to escape totalled more than 300. While some of those attempts were by the same men, it nevertheless indicates how determined and productive they were in their efforts to beat the 'escape-proof' security of Colditz Castle.

One hundred and thirty prisoners succeeded in getting away from the Castle, but were recaptured before they could get out of Germany. The number of men who actually reached the safety of their homelands was thirty. At the top of the league were the French with fourteen successful escapes, followed by the British with nine, the Dutch with six and the Poles with one.

These figures, recorded by Reinhold Eggers, a member of the Security staff who later became Security Officer, represent the highest successful escape record of any prisoner-of-war camp in Nazi

Germany. It was a remarkable achievement, considering that security at all other prisoner-of-war camps in Germany was considerably less severe and the feasibility of escape considerably greater.

For example, at a massive air force personnel prisoner-of-war camp at Sagan there were 7,000 British and Americans, guarded by a company of no more than 280 men, including a Kommandant and officers. At Colditz, however, there were at its height of occupation about 800 prisoners-of-war and there were at times, as Eggers observes in his book, *Colditz – the German Viewpoint*, as many guards as prisoners. Yet the number of escape attempts from Sagan was far less than that from Colditz.

On 15 April, 1945 Colditz Castle ceased to be a special security establishment for incorrigible escapers. On that sunny springtime Sunday morning, the town and the Castle were taken by Combat Command R of the 9th Armoured Division (Fifth Corps) of the U.S. First Army, part of the American campaign which swept through Germany to link up with British forces.

With the liberation of the British and Allied prisoners-of-war, another wretched chapter in the turbulent history of Colditz Castle had come to a close.

9

BRITISH OFFICERS IN COLDITZ

Back row left to right: 2nd Lt. Peter Allan, Queen's Own Cameron Highlanders, captured 10 June, 1940; Flt. Lt. Don Middleton, RAF, captured 18 May, 1940; Flt. Lt. Hank Wardle, RAF, captured 21 April, 1940; Lt. Tommy Elliot, Royal Northumberland Fusiliers, captured 12 June, 1940; Capt. (Rev.) Richard D. Heard, Royal Army Chaplains Department, captured 26 May, 1940; Lt. Peter Storie-Pugh, Queen's Own Royal West Kent Regiment, captured 20 May, 1940; Capt. (Rev.) Joseph C. Hobling, Royal Army Chaplains Department, captured 18 May, 1940; Lt. Geoff 'Stooge' Wardle, RN, captured 20 February, 1940; Capt. Kenneth Lockwood, the Queen's Royal Regiment, captured 21 May, 1940;

Middle row left to right: Flt. Lt. Keith Milne, RAF, captured 21 April, 1940; Capt. (Rev.) J. Ellison Platt, Royal Army Chaplains Department (attached to the 10th London CCS), captured 20 May, 1940; Lt. Col. Guy German, Leicestershire Regiment (Senior British Officer at Colditz 1941–2), captured 27 April, 1940; Capt. Harry A. V. Elliott, Irish Guards, captured 23 May, 1940; Capt. Rupert Barry, 52nd Light Infantry (the Oxfordshire and Buckinghamshire Light Infantry), captured 28 May, 1940;

Front row left to right: Lt. H. E. E. 'Teddy' Barton, Royal Army Service Corps, captured 20 May, 1940; Capt. Pat Reid, Royal Army Service Corps (Escape Officer at Colditz 1940–2), captured 27 May, 1940; Capt. Dick H. Howe, Royal Tank Regiment (Escape Officer at Colditz 1942–5), captured 26 May, 1940.

Senior officers of the various nationalities in Colditz. Left to right: Col. de Smet (Belgian); Rear Admiral J. Unrug (Polish); Lt. Gen. T. Piskor (Polish); Col. D. S. Stayner (British); Gen. le Bleu (French); Major E. Engles (Dutch).

Right: 8 August, 1941, Belgian Lieutenants Leroy and le Jeune are returned to Colditz under heavy escort. These two officers attempted a daring escape from the exercise ground. Having cleared the wire fence surrounding the area, they raced up the hill, heading for the boundary wall under a hail of bullets. Their comrades lining the Castle windows, facing the park, attempted to distract the aim of the sentries below by jeering and hurling abuse at them, which resulted in many of the guards redirecting their fire at the Castle windows. Miraculously, nobody was killed or wounded. By the time the escaping officers had reached the wall, the shooting had become so concentrated that any attempt to climb the wall would have been suicidal. Both men raised their hands above their heads and stood waiting to be collected.

CHAPTER 1
DOUBLE-CROSS DISASTER

THE SMALL BRITISH CONTINGENT of prisoners-of-war had been in Colditz Castle for less than two months before they began plotting to put Reichsmarschall Goering's escape-proof boast to the test. The first to arrive were Capt. Dick Howe, of the Royal Tank Regiment, Capt. Harry Elliott, of the Irish Guards, Capt. Rupert Barry, of the 52nd Light Infantry, Capt. Kenneth Lockwood, of the Queen's Royal Regiment, 2nd Lt. 'Peter' Allan, of the Queen's Own Cameron Highlanders, and Capt. Pat Reid, of the Royal Army Service Corps, all sent to Colditz on 10 November, 1940, after attempting to break out of Oflag VII C, a prisoner-of-war camp at Laufen, near Salzburg.

In those early days, escape ideas, techniques and materials were relatively crude and in short supply, compared with the expertise that was to develop. But the British were ready to start the ball rolling and by the Christmas of 1940, when their number had increased to sixteen, they had finalised the details of their plan, which was to dig their way out of the Castle by extending a sewer tunnel.

The entrance to the sewer was a manhole in the floor of the prisoners' canteen, which was below the British quarters. Their extension would exit in a terraced lawn just outside the south-east corner of the Castle. The terrace, fronted by a stone balustrade, dropped about forty feet to a roadway which, although heavily patrolled, led to a ravine on its far side and then the Castle park which was surrounded by nothing more than a twelve-feet high stone wall.

Over that wall was the open countryside and, they hoped, the way back to England.

The Senior British Officer, Lt. Col. Guy German, of the Leicestershire Regiment, appointed Pat Reid officer in charge of putting the plan into operation. Reid, who had played a prominent role in the

The first British arrivals at Colditz from Oflag VII C Laufen. Left to right: Capts. Harry Elliott, Rupert Barry, Pat Reid, Dick Howe, 2nd Lt. Peter Allan, Capt. Kenneth Lockwood.

escape from Oflag VII C at Laufen, was resourceful, imaginative and able to anticipate problems. He also inspired confidence in his fellow officers.

The plan came about following a conversation between Reid and a Polish orderly, one of about eighty Poles who had been captured in September 1939, and were the first prisoners-of-war to arrive at Colditz. The Pole mentioned to Reid that he had been in the prisoners' courtyard when one of two

manhole covers had been raised for whatever reason by the Germans and he had noticed small brick sewer tunnels leading off in different directions, big enough for the passage of a man.

Reid undertook an investigation. Obviously the sewers would lead under the Castle's many buildings, but were they fully accessible and did any one of them go beyond the Castle walls? If so, how far? Under the cover of darkness, Reid, accompanied by Rupert Barry, sneaked out into the courtyard and at ten-minute intervals poured pots of boiling water, heated in the prisoners' blacked-out kitchen, over the nearest manhole cover which in the sub-zero temperature was frozen hard to its iron base.

They finally managed to lever up the cover with a piece of scrap iron to reveal a shallow drop to bricked sewer outlets measuring two feet by three feet. In an instant, Reid dropped into the manhole and Barry replaced the cover, returning thirty minutes later to let Reid out. His exploration established that one of the foul, breath-wrenching tunnels led to the building which accommodated the British quarters and canteen.

It would be that tunnel Reid would finally decide upon, but there were others still to explore and it was not the obvious choice. A second tunnel led to the prisoners' kitchen within their courtyard and the third was an outfall sewer which disappeared under the iron trellis gate of the courtyard to another manhole. This appeared to be the most promising, but Reid's rising hopes were dashed by a brick wall blocking off the tunnel just beyond the outside manhole.

Night after night, he, Barry, and Dick Howe returned to try to break through the heavily cemented bricks. But their crude tools of scrap metal and canteen knives proved pathetically hopeless against the reinforced cement. So Reid's thoughts returned to the tunnel that led back to the canteen. It was worth further investigation.

Assistance from within the canteen, where the prisoners purchased their toiletries, writing materials and various other items, was a formality. For another member of the British contingent, Kenneth Lockwood, had been appointed by the Kommandant as the assistant manager and accountant. With his connivance, it was an easy affair to get regular access to the manhole cover and the tunnel beneath.

Reid found that it channelled off in two directions – one towards the manhole in the courtyard, his original starting-point, and the other curving off towards a wall of the canteen which happened to be the outside wall. That, undoubtedly, was the one to explore. It seemed to disappear under the canteen window, which looked out on to a terraced lawn and, beyond that, the roadway.

At the outside wall itself the tunnel had been blocked with stones and mortar. But closer examination of the obstruction revealed that this time they were in luck.

The mortar gave way with little resistance and, a week later, four feet of stones had been removed and hidden in the sewer tunnel leading to the courtyard. However, their rapid progress was halted when the tunnellers came across a stratum of clay which would prove almost impossible to burrow through. There was now only one practicable route the tunnel could take – upwards to the terraced lawn. From this point the escapers would have to drop the forty feet over the terrace balustrade with the aid of a bed-sheet rope and, dodging the patrolling sentries, dash across the roadway to the park.

In the meantime, Reid got busy with an ingenious idea to support the area of the lawn through which the tunnel would exit until the night of the escape. It was, in effect, a small table top on telescopic legs which was of adequate strength to take the weight of a passing soldier. The turf above would be cut round the perimeter of the table top which could be removed and replaced time and again without any apparent disturbance to the lawn.

But if emerging through the lawn without detection wasn't to be difficult enough, it was going to prove even more problematic as the result of an ill-conceived escape attempt by two Poles, whose lack of attention to detail made their efforts an inevitable disaster from the start. They broke into the canteen to saw through the bars of the window, but made such a racket they were caught red-handed. The Poles' plan was so hastily prepared that it proceeded without even the elementary insurance of a warning system provided by fellow prisoners.

The outcome was that the Senior Security Officer, Hauptmann Paul Priem, ordered the installation of a powerful searchlight to illuminate the whole terraced lawn area. It would obviously make the British prisoners' point of exit exceedingly hazardous.

To avoid a similar catastrophe, the Senior British Officer, Lt. Col. German, held an urgent meeting with the Senior Polish Officer, Gen. Tadeusz Piskor, urging close liaison between the two nationalities. This was soundly and diplomatically achieved by Guy German inviting the Polish General to select four of his officers to take part in the escape.

There were to be three more heart-stopping moments before the British could get their plan under way. The first involved Rupert Barry who was

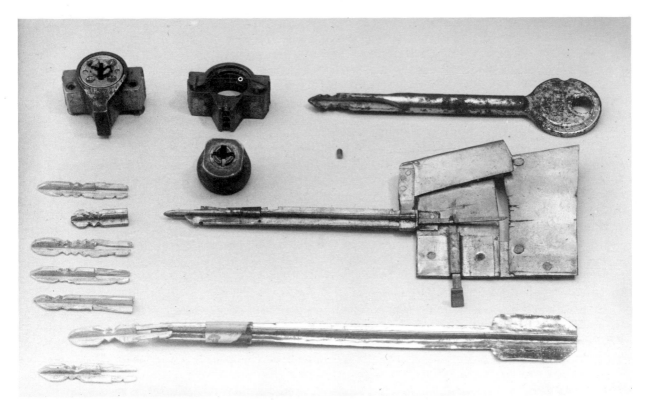

Zeiss Ikon top security cruciform locks were installed to combat lock-picking experts. The DIY lock-picking kit made from scraps of metal by Lt. Cdr. van Doorninck. Top left to right shows the complete lock, casing and barrel, one of the tiny pistons the four-sided key had to engage, and one of the keys. Centre right is van Doorninck's micrometer gauge for measuring the drop on the pistons. Left, some spare keys, and bottom right, a key holder made of tin.

caught in the spotlight while carrying sacks of food supplies for the escape from the British quarters for storage in the tunnel. He was, in fact, seen by a soldier, who was, mercifully, short-sighted. The man couldn't quite make out the movement of the blurred figure and by the time he had got nearer, Barry had disappeared. It was the kind of lucky break that often meant the difference between triumph and disaster.

The second hitch involved Reid, Howe, Barry and Lt. Geoff 'Stooge' Wardle of the Royal Navy. They were busy working in the tunnel when a party of soldiers, the worse for drink, carried out a boisterous and impromptu raid on the British quarters. But they weren't so drunk that they failed to notice four beds were empty. Their shouts were heard by Wardle, acting as look-out for his three colleagues in the tunnel. With reinforcements led by Alsatian dogs heading towards the canteen, Wardle joined the others in the tunnel, hurriedly replacing the manhole cover on his way down.

A few moments later, the soldiers were standing above them. They tried to remove the cover, unsuccessfully, since Reid was hanging on to it from below like grim death.

A roll call confirmed the absence of the four men, who could do nothing but remain for the time being in the tunnel. Barry and Howe busied themselves in building a false wall to hide the food supplies and their tunnel in case the Germans decided to return to have another attempt at removing the manhole cover. Once they had done all they could to ensure its secrecy, they returned to their quarters to face roll call the following morning and the punishment that would follow. Each man was subsequently sentenced to two weeks' solitary confinement.

The Security Officers were, not surprisingly, of the opinion that the British were planning an escape. As anticipated, soldiers did return to the canteen to remove the manhole cover. This time, without Reid's hindrance, they had no problem. But, happily, Howe and Barry had made a superb job of the false wall. Despite a careful search, the soldiers found nothing. The tunnel was safe for another day.

To eliminate the chance of the canteen manhole being used for escape purposes, four strong metal clasps were fastened in concrete around the manhole cover. They had little effect. Before the concrete could set, the British were able to loosen the clasps slightly, certainly sufficiently to remove them at will, while they would appear, when replaced, to hold the cover firm.

The third mishap happened because, once more, there had been a lack of liaison. This time it involved a Frenchman and a Pole, both of whom disappeared from a party of prisoners on its way back from daily exercise in a recreation compound set out in the Castle park. They escaped while the attentions of the soldiers, who flanked the prisoners at every few yards, was cleverly distracted long enough for the two men to dash behind a nearby wall.

It was a bold attempt that unfortunately failed. When questioned they refused to disclose how they had pulled it off, believing that the same escape ruse could be tried again, but with happier results. Instead, they fabricated a story of how they had climbed down a rope from the canteen, dropped down over the terraced lawn and disappeared into the park.

Once again, the Germans tightened security. A sentry was assigned to patrol the terraced lawn area day and night, which meant he passed the point of the tunnel exit at approximately one minute intervals. The British, now facing the possible collapse of their plan, were incensed. It appeared that their weeks of planning and tunnel excavating toil had all been for nothing. It certainly wasn't possible to get a man out of the tunnel and safely away over the balustrade in the space of a minute.

It seemed an insoluble problem. To approach one of the sentries with a bribe to look the other way was to court almost certain disaster. Nevertheless, a bribe was the only answer. The question that remained was which of the soldiers would accept one. 2nd Lt. Peter Allan and Howard Gee, a journalist attached to the Finnish International Brigade, believed they had found the ideal candidate, a man who was happy to do a bit of illegal bartering of German-produced food for Red Cross chocolate or cocoa.

So it was arranged that, at a certain time on a certain night, he would remain for ten minutes at one end of his patrol. The bribe: 500 Reichsmarks (about £34), with a down payment of 100 Reichsmarks. The balance would be dropped out of a window one hour after the escape had taken place.

The deal was done, but it was to lead directly to disaster.

Reid meanwhile was concerned with how to get thirteen officers into the canteen which now, thanks to the Pole and the Frenchman, had special high security locks fitted. These were cruciform locks which could only be opened by what looked like a four-sided Yale key. Known as Zeiss Ikon locks, they seemed impossible to crack. Reid's solution was to have himself locked in the canteen by Lockwood shortly before the escape was due to take place and dismantle the lock from the inside. It would be re-fitted by Capt. Cyril Lewthwaite, of the Warwickshires, who would remain behind to replace the manhole cover and the metal clasps and to remove any tell-tale signs of escape.

The appointed day for the escape was 29 May, 1941. The day before Reid hid in a canteen cupboard. In the lunch interval, when the canteen was locked for two hours, he let himself out and disappeared into the tunnel. He made a final check of the exit, broke through the false wall and took the food supplies, which were to be distributed to the escapers before they left the British quarters, and returned to the cupboard where he remained until the canteen was opened by a soldier. With the help of other prisoners creating a diversion, Reid nipped out of the cupboard and returned to his quarters.

29 May greeted the prisoners with torrential rain. It continued throughout the day to encompass the Castle in a grey, seemingly impenetrable curtain of mist. It was no bad omen. It would mean that the sentries would be keeping their heads down, cursing the rain, their alertness blunted.

The thirteen officers were to leave their quarters in darkness after evening roll call. Wearing their civilian clothes under their uniforms, they ambled out as calmly as possible to the prisoners' inner courtyard. Lt. Col. Guy German, the Senior British Officer, took up his position in front of the British prisoners-of-war. He was included in the escape squad and, with his escape clothes under his uniform, had apparently put on considerable weight.

The Germans went through the mechanical roll call count. Everything went normally. The prisoners were dismissed and returned to their respective quarters. As they walked off in different directions, the four Polish officers selected to escape ducked quickly into the British quarters.

Right: The entrance to the canteen tunnel. Inset: The exit of the canteen tunnel below the window.

A jubiliant Security staff pose with the 150 lb haul of Red Cross food picked up from the canteen tunnel. On the far right is Capt. Hans Lange, Security Officer at Colditz from 1939 to October 1943, on his right is Capt. Vent, in charge of the parcels office, next to him is NCO Teicher, the officer who caused Lt. Storie-Pugh some anxious moments with a shaking revolver.

The sentry had been briefed earlier that afternoon. Reid made his final visit to the canteen. While Lockwood diverted the attention of a soldier, he hid inside the cupboard. Shortly after the canteen was locked for the night, Reid emerged and quickly dismantled the cruciform lock. There was nothing more he could do but wait. With the arrival of his twelve colleagues, the manhole cover was lifted clear and Reid lowered himself down. He was followed by Rupert Barry and the other officers who disappeared one by one into the tunnel until there

was only the thirteenth man, Lewthwaite, remaining in the canteen. Discarded British officers' uniforms lay on the floor. It was one of his jobs to conceal them in the cupboard and remove them the next day.

In the tunnel, Reid cut round the table top which had been supporting the lawn above. The rain poured through, running down his arms and saturating his clothing. As he pushed out the neatly-cut square of lawn and laid it to one side, the cold night air hit his face and he saw the Castle wall brilliantly floodlit.

With a shove from Barry, he climbed up on to the lawn. Barry passed up Reid's rucksack and began to haul himself out of the tunnel in turn. At that moment Reid glanced up at the Castle Wall. What he saw made him go rigid with horror. There against the wall, next to the shadow of his crouching

figure, was another – of a man standing over him.

Before Reid could move, the quiet of the night was shattered by the command: 'Hands up! Hands up!'

A German officer was standing just a few feet away with a gun levelled at him. Soldiers appeared from every direction. Another officer was at the hole in an instant with his gun aimed down the tunnel. Reid was rapidly frog-marched away, while the men below ground tried, like trapped rats, to scurry back down the tunnel, vainly hoping to get safely to their quarters. But the Germans were waiting for them, smugly counting them off as they emerged through the canteen manhole entrance. The prisoners, grimly disappointed, could do nothing but stand silently against the wall of the canteen while the elated Security Officers checked the tunnel.

Lt. Peter Storie-Pugh, of the Queen's Own Royal West Kent Regiment, remembers an NCO called Teicher (nicknamed Tiger), who was pointing his gun at him. Tiger was so unnerved by the drama of it all, and his hand was shaking so much that Storie-Pugh seriously believed a bullet would cut him down at any moment, and he, at least, was grateful when the prisoners were taken to the Kommandantur for questioning.

The Germans had obviously been aware of the proposed tunnel escape for some while. The sentry had informed the Kommandant of the bribe. The soldier was handsomely rewarded, being allowed to keep the 100 Reichsmarks, promoted and awarded the War Service Cross. He was also, for his own safety, quickly transferred. The thwarting of the British left the Germans cock-a-hoop. It was one up to Colditz Castle.

French Officer Lt. Alain le Ray, the first prisoner to escape from Oflag IV C Colditz. 11 April, 1941. Lt. le Ray made his escape on the way back from the park where the prisoners exercised. Waiting until the column rounded a curve in the path, placing a blind spot between him and the nearest guards, he leapt down a short embankment and into a vaulted cellar below a row of terraced houses, normally used as an air-raid shelter. The guards saw nothing and the column of prisoners continued on into the Castle. Lt. le Ray realised that he had only minutes to make good his escape, his friends had promised to try and cause a diversion at the count, but if they failed the dogs and guards would be on his trail before he could even get out of the park. The Lieutenant made his way cautiously back along the path, only to discover three Germans playing football in the barbed wire enclosure. He couldn't possibly pass without being seen, so he was forced to retrace his steps to the cellar. Half an hour passed without any alarm and le Ray knew his friends must have succeeded. But the next roll call would be at 6.00 p.m., in an hour's time, so he had to make his move. This time his luck was in. He made his way swiftly through the park to the perimeter wall, and freedom.

I n May 1941 Lts. Surmanowicz and Chmiel, two Polish officers, attempted an escape that for sheer audacity and daring earned them the admiration of prisoners and guards alike. The Poles were serving solitary confinement in the courtyard punishment cells. Each cell bordered on to a corridor, which in turn had its main door opening on to the prisoners' yard. Late one evening, working to a pre-arranged plan, they picked the locks on their cells and the main door and crept out into the courtyard.

Their comrades, watching from a window high above in the Polish quarters, quickly lowered a sheet rope and each officer was hoisted to a ledge some forty feet above the ground.

After regaining their breath, Surmanowicz and Chmiel, keeping a tight hold on the rope, slowly edged their precipitous way along until they came to the sloping guard-house roof. Climbing up this, they dropped through a skylight into a deserted attic, whose window, 120 feet from the ground, overlooked the fields surrounding the

Castle. Securing one end of the rope to a beam, they lowered the remainder through the open window, breathing a sigh of relief to discover their calculations had been correct and the bed sheets, so generously donated by their comrades for the rope's manufacture, not only reached the ground but left them a few yards spare.

Clambering through the window the Poles began their strenuous climb down the face of the Castle. All was going well and the officers had covered approximately fifty feet in

the descent, when Chmiel, who was wearing heavy nailed boots, scraped the wall as he was passing the window of a room occupied by duty guards. A suspicious duty officer, thrusting his head out of the window, spotted the two escapees and raised the alarm.

As usual at such moments pandemonium reigned. The screaming voice of the duty officer could be heard calling for the Riot Squad. The thunderous sound of sentries' boots as some rushed up to the attic to cut off retreat and others down to the ground to await the prisoners' arrival, was added to the verbal barrage from sentries crowding the open windows. One, red-faced and over excited, was pointing a shaking pistol in the Poles' direction and ordering them to raise their hands! An order that Surmanowicz and Chmiel, clinging like grim death to a rope eighty feet from the ground, chose to ignore.

Right: A German sentry takes a worm's eye view of the escape route taken by Lts. Surmanowicz and Chmiel. Above: *The rope left by Lts. Surmanowicz and Chmiel could be clearly seen from the town.*

Front row, left to right: Flt. Lt. Patrick Dickenson, Sqn. Ldr. Geoffrey Stevenson, Flt. Lt. Vincent Parker, Group Capt. Douglas Bader, Sqn. Ldr. Malcolm McColm, Sqn. Ldr. Charles Lockett, Flt. Lt. Dominic Bruce.
Back row, left to right: Flt. Lt. Jack Best, Flt. Lt. Norman Forbes, Flt. Lt. Jack Zafouk, Flt. Lt. Vincent Flynn, Flt. Lt. Peter van Rood, Flt. Lt. Dan Halifax, Flt. Lt. Don Donaldson, Flt. Lt. Don Thom, Flt. Lt. Keith Milne, Flt. Lt. Don Middleton, Flt. Lt. Bill Goldfinch.

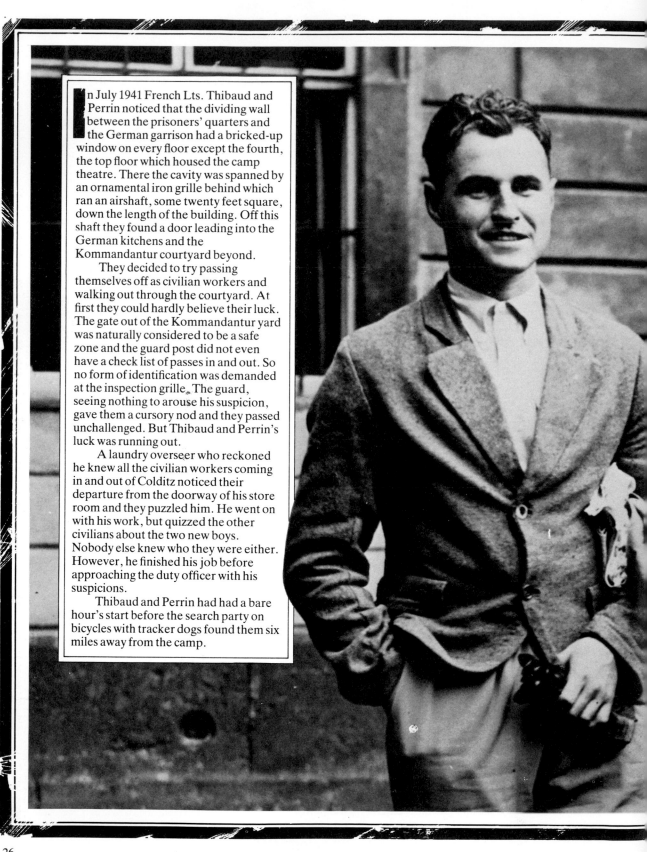

In July 1941 French Lts. Thibaud and Perrin noticed that the dividing wall between the prisoners' quarters and the German garrison had a bricked-up window on every floor except the fourth, the top floor which housed the camp theatre. There the cavity was spanned by an ornamental iron grille behind which ran an airshaft, some twenty feet square, down the length of the building. Off this shaft they found a door leading into the German kitchens and the Kommandantur courtyard beyond.

They decided to try passing themselves off as civilian workers and walking out through the courtyard. At first they could hardly believe their luck. The gate out of the Kommandantur yard was naturally considered to be a safe zone and the guard post did not even have a check list of passes in and out. So no form of identification was demanded at the inspection grille. The guard, seeing nothing to arouse his suspicion, gave them a cursory nod and they passed unchallenged. But Thibaud and Perrin's luck was running out.

A laundry overseer who reckoned he knew all the civilian workers coming in and out of Colditz noticed their departure from the doorway of his store room and they puzzled him. He went on with his work, but quizzed the other civilians about the two new boys. Nobody else knew who they were either. However, he finished his job before approaching the duty officer with his suspicions.

Thibaud and Perrin had had a bare hour's start before the search party on bicycles with tracker dogs found them six miles away from the camp.

CHAPTER 2

C'EST LA VIE

THE FRENCH PRISONERS' tunnel was the most ambitious underground escape project ever undertaken in Colditz Castle. It was a remarkable feat of engineering, constructed under the harshest of conditions and accomplished with nothing more than the crudest tools.

For eight months they toiled, scraping, digging and cutting through stone-hard timbers, rock foundations and tons of earth. The Germans knew, for most of that time, what the French were up to because it was impossible to suppress the noise, but they were powerless to check the tunnel's progress because its entrance was so cunningly concealed. The only concession the French made to the search efforts of the Germans was to cease work whenever a warning signal alerted them to soldiers in the immediate proximity.

Work on the tunnel began in June 1941. It is uncertain who first conceived the idea, but the original tunnel committee consisted of nine men. They were: Lt. Roger Madin (Artillery); Flt. Lt. Léonce Godfrin; Lts. Jean Brejoux, Jean Gambero, Bernard Cazaumayo and Georges Dielder (Infantry). The other French officers were Jean Chaudrut, Edgar Barres and Lt. Paille.

The tunnel's route was worked out by first deciding on the safest place to exit. They agreed on the east side of the Castle park. It was calculated they would have to excavate to a final depth of just over twenty-seven feet, which would mean, at certain stages, cutting through the Castle's medieval rock foundations. Working back to the nearest point to the French quarters would mean starting from the Castle's cellars. But between the cellars and their quarters, on the first, second, third and fourth floors of a building in the north-west corner of the prisoner's courtyard, were the ground-floor parcels office, stores and infirmary.

The problem was solved by the experiences of Lts. Cazaumayo and Paille who, less than a year earlier, had got into a clock tower at the corner of the building in which the French were housed and discovered its shaft went down to ground level. They had gained entry through a small door – there was one on each floor – which gave maintenance access for the clock's mechanism. This had long been removed, but the doors, at the ends of the corridors, had been left intact. After that incident, they were quickly bricked up.

Above: Col. Schmidt, Kommandant of Oflag IV C Colditz Castle, 1940–August 1942. Right: Capt. Reinhold Eggers, Camp Officer at Oflag IV C Colditz from August 1940 until February 1944 when he became Security Officer until the Americans liberated the Castle in April 1945.

This time the French discovered an easier, and safer, way of getting inside the tower. They examined the attics above them and found that beams used to seal the top of the tower could easily be removed, exposing the shaft. The removal many

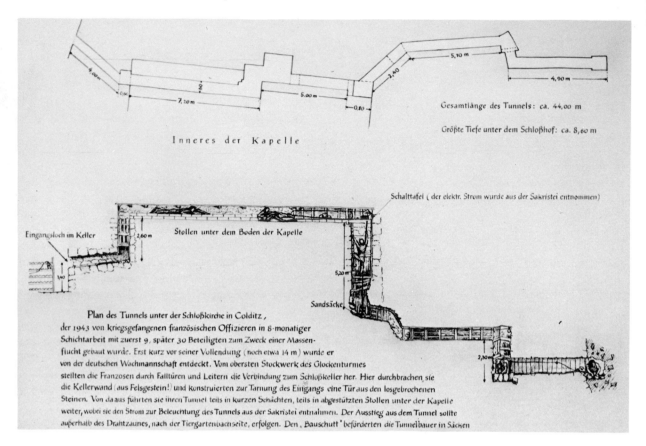

Inneres der Kapelle

Gesamtlänge des Tunnels: ca. 44,00 m

Größte Tiefe unter dem Schloßhof: ca. 8,60 m

Schalttafel (der elektr. Strom wurde aus der Sakristei entnommen)

Eingangsloch im Keller

Stollen unter dem Boden der Kapelle

Sandsäcke

Plan des Tunnels unter der Schloßkirche in Colditz,
der 1943 von kriegsgefangenen französischen Offizieren in 8-monatiger
Schichtarbeit mit zuerst 9, später 30 Beteiligten zum Zweck einer Massen-
flucht gebaut wurde. Erst kurz vor seiner Vollendung (noch etwa 14 m) wurde er
von der deutschen Wachmannschaft entdeckt. Vom obersten Stockwerk des Glockenturmes
stellten die Franzosen durch Falltüren und Leitern die Verbindung zum Schloßkeller her. Hier durchbrachen sie
die Kellerwand (aus Felsgestein!) und konstruierten zur Tarnung des Eingangs eine Tür aus den losgebrochenen
Steinen. Von da aus führten sie ihren Tunnel teils in kurzen Schächten, teils in abgestützten Stollen unter der Kapelle
weiter, wobei sie den Strom zur Beleuchtung des Tunnels aus der Sakristei entnahmen. Der Ausstieg aus dem Tunnel sollte
außerhalb des Drahtzaunes, nach der Tiergartenbachseite, erfolgen. Den „Bauschutt" beförderten die Tunnelbauer in Säcken.

years earlier of the clock weights and cables provided ample room for the French to climb 110 feet down a dark rope ladder to ground level, where they could then dig down through the arched roof of the cellars below.

The tunnel route was now considered to be a feasible proposition, so the job of amassing the necessary tools and equipment began. One of their main requirements was an endless supply of bed boards to shore up the tons of earth beneath which they would be working. Breaking into the cellars was a comparatively easy affair and there were more than enough Frenchmen willing to help haul the sacks of debris up into the spacious attic above their quarters, working every available minute between the daily roll calls.

The entrance to the tunnel was started in a wall at the end of the cellar and approximately four feet from the ground. From the large stones removed from the wall a false door was made and cleverly hinged on a steel pivot so that it could be quickly opened and closed in an emergency. A supply of grit, sand and clay, which made an excellent mortar identical in colour to surrounding mortar, was always readily available.

The Germans made a drawing of the tunnel.

The tunnel proceeded horizontally for about thirteen feet. It then rose seven feet, sharply vertical, which took them directly under the floor of the prisoners' chapel. The chapel was twenty-three feet long, a level stretch which added considerably to the rapid progress of the tunnel. It was also possible to provide lighting for the tunnel by wiring into the chapel's electricity supply. This was installed by Lt. Roger Madin, a skilled electrician, with the assistance of the Frenchmen's spiritual adviser, Curé Jeanjean, who ensured that Madin was allowed to work undisturbed. While a 'worshipper' was always on hand if a guard came near, to alert his colleagues beneath him with a signal which cut warning flashes into their lighting system and temporarily silenced the noise of the sacks of debris being hauled along on a pulley system of wooden sledges.

For months the Germans had realised that the French were involved in a massive escape enterprise. During a search of the French quarters on the floor beneath the attic, they noticed that one of the huge ceiling beams was beginning to crack. It wasn't difficult to establish the cause. Under the inner eaves in the attic above, they discovered tons of debris and rock, including samples of porphyry containing crystal which had obviously come from a considerable depth beneath the castle. It was equally obvious, judging from the quantity, that it was from a tunnel of some length which had been under construction for many weeks.

The Germans couldn't understand, however, how the French were getting almost unhindered twenty-four-hour access to their tunnel. A third daily roll call was introduced, in an attempt to disrupt the tunnelling, and two NCOs were ordered to patrol the prisoners' courtyard and quarters as a psychological deterrent. The French replied by assigning colleagues to follow them casually, and give the signal if they got anywhere near the tunnel area.

The Castle security forces were tormented by

The prisoners' chapel on the east side of the Castle. The French tunnel ran left to right underneath the altar.

the sheer arrogance of the French who, working in the dead of night, were aware that the reverberating noise of their tunnelling could be heard by the Germans, but their confidence in its undetectable entrance was total.

Kommandant Schmidt felt it was high time that the Oberkommando der Wehrmacht in Berlin, the German Army High Command, was informed. High-ranking personnel were despatched from Berlin and the Army Command H.Q. in Dresden to deal with the impertinent Frenchmen.

Their arrival in September 1941, reinforced by additional personnel from neighbouring prisoner-of-war camps, heralded the biggest search of the

Castle ever undertaken. The prisoners were to be kept in the courtyard until the tunnel was found. Every corner was searched, every square inch examined, every wall tapped for an unexpected echo. Floorboards were removed, every attic of the buildings round the courtyard was scrupulously inspected, so were the prisoners' kitchens, theatre and even the chapel. Especial attention was centred on the French quarters. Every conceivable, and inconceivable, area was probed. The cellars were investigated with manic thoroughness. By late afternoon, the searchers had found a treasure trove in escape equipment, forged documents and clothing, which had been stored for future escapes, but not a clue to the tunnels

And the French dug on. There were seven, sixteen inches square, oak timbers supporting the chapel floorboards which had become steel-hard over the centuries and the Frenchmen hacked through them with nothing more than knives from the kitchen. It was a task that had tested their determination to the limit, taking several weeks of agonisingly frustrating effort.

At the end of the chapel, the tunnel dropped sixteen feet which was necessary for the tunnellers to get under the Castle's foundations. At the bottom of this shaft, they veered forty-five degrees downhill to the left for about seven feet. They then straightened out for sixteen feet and dropped sharply again for another seven feet. They were now outside the Castle wall and the tunnel was making rapid progress through soil for about sixteen feet. Another fifty feet and it would be finished.

By now, it was January 1942. Eight months had passed since the French had shifted the first sack of earth from the floor of the clock tower, and the Germans were increasingly exasperated by their failure to locate the tunnel.

But time was running out . . .

The Security Officer, Reinhold Eggers, went over in his mind for the umpteenth time all the places that could offer cover for a tunnel entrance. The cellars below the French quarters offered, of course, the logical answer, but they had been searched so many times they had to be ruled out. Eggers' thoughts strayed to the clock tower. He idly recalled the day, almost a year earlier, when two Frenchmen had been caught in the tower's shaft. That was one place they hadn't searched. It was on 15 January that Eggers ordered one of his sergeants, Feldwebel Gephard, to take a couple of soldiers and examine the clock tower.

Above left: Beyond the wine racks the tunnel goes out through the cellar wall.

Above right: The parallel shaft leading back towards the entrance in the cellar. The matting sledge with its bed-sheet pulling rope can be seen in the centre of the photograph.

Facing, top far left: One of the clock-tower chambers leading to the cellar. On the right is the iron ladder used to gain entrance to the roof, on the left a sack containing rubble. One of the sleeves that had housed the clock chains and weights can be seen bottom centre.

Left, top: Rock dug from the Castle foundations piled into a recess in one of the clock-tower chambers.

Bottom far left: The end of the shaft below the sacristy. The wires on the left were for the lighting circuit and signalling devices.

Bottom, left: The shaft leading down under the sacristy to the Castle's original foundations.

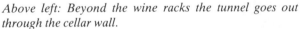

With the aid of the soldiers, Gephard removed the heavy timbers from across the top of the shaft. A beam of light from his powerful torch sliced through the darkness. That instant, Gephard was sure he heard a noise coming from the depths.

With typical German thoroughness, Eggers had instructed Gephard to take with him a small youth who could be lowered down the shaft. A rope was quickly tied round his waist. Slowly and noiselessly, he was lowered down into the darkness. A moment later, the youth's voice shattered the silence.

'Da ist jemand dort!' he cried. (There is someone there.)

It was the beginning of the end for the French tunnelling masterpiece.

The noise that Gephard had heard was caused by one of the three Frenchmen taking sacks of debris from the rope pulley system to be hidden later in the attic.

The French, in blinding panic, smashed their way through the shaft wall, shattering the privacy of a Belgian army Major, Baron Lindkerke, who was basking in the luxury of a hot bath.

Gephard sent the soldiers storming down to the floors below, but by the time the Germans had located the room through which they had made the exit, the Frenchmen had disappeared.

The Germans now knew that the cellars were the key to the tunnel. Once again they were searched in painstaking fashion, but once again, incredibly, the entrance could not be found. Eggers ordered a soldier to be put on duty in the cellars while he and his senior officers retired to consider their next course of action.

They needn't have bothered. The soldier solved the mystery. With a piece of metal, he tapped random parts of the wall. By chance, he struck one of the stones of the bogus door. The surrounding home-made mortar had, unbeknown to the French, come loose. The stone moved slightly. The soldier removed it with ease. The tunnel had been discovered.

The French were convinced that they had been betrayed by one of their countrymen who had been transferred to another prisoner-of-war camp at Elsterhorst, but this is denied in the account by Eggers in his book, *Colditz – the German View-*

point.

The final blow for the French was a demand by the German authorities for money to repair the damage caused to the clock tower, attics and chapel sub-floor. It would cost, according to a local contractor, 12,000 Reichsmarks – nearly £1,000 – to repair. The estimate also included the cost of labour to remove the tons of debris.

Kommandant Schmidt tried to raise the money by imposing a levy on prisoners' pay, which was at half their home rate of pay. It caused a tremendous outcry from the other nationalities. The Oberkommando der Wehrmacht was called in to decide

One of the twenty-one Frenchmen who worked in the tunnel was Lt. Edgar Duque, of the 160th Regiment of Artillery. He said: 'It was truly like a hell hole down there. I think it was an incredible effort and deserved the reward of success. I assure you it took a lot of courage to work in that tunnel.'

Like many of his colleagues, Duque was transferred from Colditz to Oflag X C at Lübeck shortly after the tunnel was discovered. The French had known that many of them were due to be transferred any day from Colditz Castle, which was why they had worked so feverishly to finish their tunnel.

But the Germans won – by just forty-eight feet.

With the chapel still closed for repairs after the discovery of the French tunnel, the Catholic community celebrates Easter 1942 in the prisoners' yard. The closed door of the canteen can be seen to the left of the altar.
Below: 16 January, 1942. The French tunnel has been discovered. The German High Command are so elated they send special emissary Mutschmann, Gauleiter of Saxony, to inspect the camp. Stepping out of the doorway fourth from the left is Mutschmann, on his left Col. Schmidt (Kommandant).
Bottom: Edgar Duque, Paris 1979.

the issue. Officials agreed that it was a collective punishment and, in the circumstances, was against a condition of the Geneva Convention. They ruled against the Kommandant.

However, Schmidt finally won the day. He used the Convention to argue a case that the money could come from the prisoners' canteen profits as such profit could be used 'for the benefit of the prisoners'. He claimed, and was this time supported by the OKW officials, that it was to the prisoners' benefit that the attic roofs, damaged by the weight of the tunnel debris, should not collapse on them or the chapel floor beneath them.

FLUSHED OUT – FROM THE GERMAN LAVATORIES

ON THE RARE OCCASIONS the German Security officials became aware of an escape plot, it was often their policy to allow it to continue unhindered, as long as circumstances permitted them to keep a check on progress and total control over the outcome. Better, in their view, to have the prisoners labouring busily on a plan known than one unknown; and last minute failure dealt the severest blow to the prisoners' morale, dampening their enthusiasm for further escape attempts for some considerable time.

It was decided to play such a cat-and-mouse game with the British who, without a great deal of attention to finer detail, proposed an escape route through the Kommandantur, a huge building in the outer courtyard which contained the office of the Kommandant, administrative offices and senior officers' quarters.

The British at that time were living on the first floor of a building which accommodated the prisoners' canteen and which, at the rear, adjoined the Kommandantur building, which formed a substantial part of the Castle's eastern face. The plan was to break through the adjoining wall and then, dressed as civilians, climb through a window on the eastern face, drop down on to the surrounding road which led to the Castle park and from there make for the open countryside.

As many men as possible would make the attempt. But the plan was fraught with problems to which the British had no answers.

They would be breaking into territory about which they knew dangerously little. Without some knowledge of the activities and movements of the soldiers and officers and a plan of the building's lay-out, escaping through one of its windows would be hazardous enough, but finding one in the first place without being spotted was to run an impossible risk.

The best that can be said of the escape is that it took place during the early days, when escape technique and skills were in their infancy. It is highly unlikely that it would have gone ahead later when their tactics became considerably more sophisticated in planning and execution.

The plan developed from the conversation a Polish army Cadet Officer, Anthony Karpf, nicknamed 'The Fish', had with Flt. Lt. Francis 'Errol'

Flynn. The young Pole told Flynn that during a visit to his Dutch friends, who had previously occupied the British quarters, he had heard the flushing of toilets through the adjoining wall. Flynn, realising its potential, discussed the matter in greater detail with Pat Reid who at that time was the British Escape Officer. Reid agreed that it was an escape idea worth exploring further.

It took two-man teams forty-eight hours to remove the eighteen-inch-thick brickwork, leaving the plaster intact on the lavatory side of the wall. Through a pin-prick hole they could see that the cubicle door was high enough to act as a screen. To the left was the lavatory bowl.

But even at this early stage their activities were known to the Germans. A soldier, on night duty at the Castle's telephone switchboard, heard the rhythmic scraping of metal against brickwork when he was visiting the lavatory. So the Germans took the precaution of drilling a small hole through the door of the guards' quarters which directly faced the lavatories. It provided a superb spy-hole and a constant watch was kept on the lavatory door.

The soldiers and officers were instructed to use the lavatories as normal, and two days later, a Security Officer reported the appearance of the pin-prick spy-hole in one of the cubicles. Clearly, the British were almost ready to make their move.

It happened on Sunday, 31 July, 1941. The British knew that there was little activity in the Kommandantur and administrative offices over the weekend and Sunday was likely to find the Colditz personnel at their most relaxed.

The first two men to climb through the hole were 2nd Lt. Peter Allan and Flt. Lt. Francis Flynn. Within seconds they were across the lavatory floor, through the door – and into the arms of the Chief Security Officer, two NCOs and six rifle-wielding soldiers.

One of the NCOs, named Grünert, who was in charge of the Castle's parcels office, was a man with a warped sense of humour. At his suggestion, Allan

Above left: The German viewpoint. The lavatory bowl has been moved forward to allow more of the escape hole to be seen in the photograph.

A mixed bag caught escaping through the wall of the German lavatory. Back row, left to right: 2nd Lt. Allan; Belgian Lt. Verkest; Lt. Hyde-Thompson; Flt. Lts. Middleton and Flynn; Polish Cadet Officer Karpf. Front row, Lts. Cheetham, Elliot, Barton; Belgian Lt. Arcque.

and Flynn were stripped of their civilian clothes which were then donned by two soldiers who were instructed to walk towards the park, by the route the British were watching from their quarters to see if their plan was working. The British were ecstatic and, two by two, they climbed through the hole at precisely five-minute intervals.

All together five pairs of the prisoners were taken into custody. The charade finally came to an end after the Senior British Officers became suspicious about the fate of the men who had followed Allan and Flynn. They had seen those two walking towards the park, but what had happened to the rest? They held back from sending any more men through the hole. In reply the Chief Security Officer despatched the NCO Tiger Teicher, to investigate. He peered round the lavatory cubicle door . . . to be met by the face of a startled British prisoner peeping through the hole.

Soldiers waiting outside in the courtyard were then given a signal to storm the British quarters. The British prisoners still due to escape had managed to get out of their civilian clothes, but these had been hurriedly stashed inside a stove and were easily found by the Germans. The ten men who walked into the arms of the Germans were Allan and Flynn, Flt. Lt. Don Middleton, Lt. Tommy Elliot, of the Royal Northumberland Fusiliers, Lt. Alan Cheetham, of the Royal Navy, Lt. John Hyde-Thompson of the Durham Light Infantry, Lt. Teddy Barton, RASC, and Belgian Lts. Arcque and Verkest, and Polish Cadet Officer Anthony Karpf, whose conversation with Flynn had inspired the plan in the first place.

Karpf was later transferred to another prisoner-of-war camp in Lübeck and from there he did manage to escape, finally making his way to England and then to Scotland where he became a successful businessman in Glasgow. Ruefully he admits: 'The tactic of the Germans in allowing us to continue while they obviously knew what we were up to had a very demoralising effect. It made you think they knew everything we were doing. It shattered the confidence of some of the men, which was precisely what the Germans hoped for.'

Above: The Censor room. Right: The Security Office.
Far right: The view from the British quarters showing the German lavatories through the hole in the wall.

Whenever security had to search prisoners' quarters, they were confronted by a mass of books, clothing, shoes, musical instruments, bric-a-brac of every shape and size. Most POWs became magpies after a prolonged period of captivity. The British quarters were considered the worst. In order to get all this superfluous paraphernalia tidied out of the way, the Germans provided empty Red Cross tea chests and this was Flt. Lt. Dominic (left) Bruce's big chance.

The Senior British Officer, Col. Todd, persuaded the Germans it would save a lot of time and motion if these chests were packed in the prisoners' own quarters, rather than the courtyard, and it was the work of moments to pack Flt. Lt. Bruce into one and lightly nail on the lid. The cases were then trundled over to a third-floor store room in the Kommandantur.

Next day Colditz received a visit from General Wolff, officer in charge of prisoners-of-war, Army district No. 4, Dresden. He was quite complimentary about the efficiency of the security arrangements and left at midday. One hour later a civilian reported seeing a blue and white bed-sheet rope hanging down from the store-room window (far left). The rope could be seen from the main gate. How the General had missed it they never knew. They did not need to call a roll call to discover who had escaped. Bruce had left them a message – '*Die Luft in Colditz gefällt mir nicht mehr! Auf Wiedersehen!* Ex P.W. Flying Officer Bruce.' (The air in Colditz no longer pleases me! Till we meet again!) Flt. Lt. Bruce was caught a week later in Danzig.

THE CHOCOLATE CAR

HOW MUCH IS A CAR WORTH – in bars of chocolate? It is, in any rational set of circumstances, a ridiculous question to be dismissed without further consideration. But Colditz Castle and the uncertainty of war was not an environment that necessarily encouraged rational thought. For that question was posed in all seriousness by Lt. John Hyde-Thompson, of the Durham Light Infantry, to a number of his fellow officers when conversation drifted towards the luxuries of life – such as bars of chocolate, for which Hyde-Thompson had developed a great passion.

Their conversation came to a sudden halt when he solemnly announced: 'I have a car in London which has never been on the road. It is a Citroën, and I am willing to part with that car in the future for chocolate in the present.' It was an offer which, even in a daily atmosphere where the unpredictable or zany event was not uncommon, startled the most imperturbable amongst them. It took several moments and a repetition of the offer before the prisoners realised it was being made in all earnestness.

So the bids began at what must rank as one of the strangest auctions of all time. Hyde-Thompson rejected the early bids with contempt. Then, Lt. John Rawson, an extrovert of a character, joined in with a stupendous bid that none of the others had a chance of matching.

'Well,' said twenty-four-year-old Rawson, who was serving with the Australian Expeditionary Forces, 'let's stop buggering about. I will bid four-and-a-quarter *pounds* of chocolate for the car.'

The Aussie's bid had almost the same seismic effect as the original announcement of the auction. But Hyde-Thompson was sceptical that Rawson had that much chocolate stored away. He turned towards Lt. David 'Hamish' Hamilton of the Royal Artillery for confirmation. Hamilton, who knew that Rawson had been stock-piling Red Cross supplies of chocolate for bartering purposes, assured him that Rawson could back up his bid. Hyde-Thompson closed the auction. The transaction was recorded by Lt. Alan 'Black' Campbell, of the Royal Artillery, who had been a successful advocate before the war.

Hamilton recalls that the wording of the agreement began: 'Whereas in consideration of payment of four-and-a-quarter pounds of chocolate . . .' It was duly signed by Hyde-Thompson and Rawson. After the war, when Hyde-Thompson's banquet of chocolate was no more than a sweet-toothed memory, Rawson collected his Citroën which he then sold before returning to Australia.

Recalled Hamilton: 'The whole episode no doubt seems bizarre in the extreme to anyone who cannot imagine the unpredictability of the situation we were in. The future of us all was of some concern and doubt. A car which might never have been seen again was, to Hyde-Thompson, something worth disposing of in exchange for a commodity that was available there and then. In those kind of surroundings, a lot of things happen that aren't logical. There was not a great deal that made much sense.'

BAGGED - BY AN INFORMER

CHAPTER 5

COLLABORATION with the German authorities in Colditz Castle was extremely rare. Only two Frenchmen and a Pole ever gave cause to be suspected by their countrymen and they were hastily removed after their senior officers made it clear to the Kommandant that the health of the suspected informers would suffer greatly if they were not transferred within twenty-four hours.

Very few quislings became so voluntarily; the majority were enlisted through fear, not for their own safety, but for that of their families. By reading the prisoners' letters in which hopes and fears would be revealed, it was an easy matter to discover who would be most likely to crack and when.

Standard 'hot' and 'cold' psychological tactics were used to manipulate them: sympathy, understanding, the kind gesture, a special privilege or two; then without warning, the sense of well-being would be shattered by brutality, isolation and threats. And the ultimate threat would be the removal of a loved one to a concentration camp. In such circumstances, it is easy to understand how a man could come to betray his fellow prisoners, even though by so doing he would be putting his own life in danger from men waging their own secret war against the Germans.

It is not possible to say how many escape attempts from Colditz were sabotaged by undetected informers; certainly very few, indeed. But it was strongly believed that one Dutch attempt was foiled because of a Polish collaborator.

The escape plan was master-minded by Capt. Machiel van den Heuvel, of the Royal Netherlands Indies Army, who was the Escape Officer of the Dutch contingent. It was inspired by weekly visits of

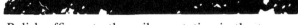

Dutch Cadet Officer Charlie Linck poses for another picture destined for the Castle museum.

Polish officers to the railway station in the town of Colditz. The Poles, who were despised by the Germans – an emotion well reciprocated by the Poles – were appointed orderlies to carry out menial tasks, such as collecting under guard large bags of parcels and Red Cross supplies from the station, loading them on to a horse-drawn cart and delivering them to the Castle.

The guards accompanying the delivery never checked the number of bags that were dropped off at the Castle. They would not know how many bags, destined for German soldiers stationed in barracks some distance from the Castle, remained on the cart.

It was unlikely, therefore, van den Heuvel believed, that the guards would notice another one – containing a Dutch prisoner-of-war.

Van den Heuvel was sure that it would be a simple task for the human cargo to be loaded on to the cart while the guards were distracted by a simple diversion. Once outside the Castle, the Dutchman would have ample time to cut himself free of the bag before the cart reached the barracks and make his escape.

The plan was simple, involved little preparation and could be put into operation at a moment's notice. It had all the ingredients for success. The Poles were willing to co-operate. The Dutchman

chosen for the mission was a young Cadet Officer called Charlie Linck. He was just five feet five inches and weighed fifty-seven kilos, small and light enough to be hidden in a bag and thrown hurriedly on to the cart without too much effort.

Escape liaison between the Dutch and the British was by now a common occurrence. The two nationalities co-existed extremely well and frequently assisted each other with escape intelligence and materials. This occasion was no exception and it was agreed that a British prisoner-of-war would accompany Linck. That man, also of diminutive stature, was Flt. Lt. Francis Flynn.

The necessary documentation – identity papers, work permits and German money – were soon made available. Civilian clothing for the two men was minimal. The attempt was to take place in the spring of 1942. Just sweaters and trousers would be adequate.

On the appointed day, Linck and Flynn were given a final briefing by van den Heuvel. The plan was so simple, it was hardly necessary, but the meticulous van den Heuvel was the last man to leave anything to chance.

The Polish orderly played little part in driving the parcel-laden cart over the moat bridge and in to the Castle. The old, dapple grey horse, sluggish with age, had travelled the journey so many times that he needed no direction. Slowly, the small convoy, flanked either side by a German soldier, creaked its way under the clock tower entrance, across the outer courtyard and into the inner courtyard where the old horse came to a halt outside the parcels office.

The driver and his fellow orderly got down and walked round to the rear of the cart. The bags were unloaded and carried into the parcels office at an unhurried pace. There was no urgency. To the orderlies it was a monotonous task, and to the guards it was an event that filled them with boredom and total disinterest. The Polish orderlies were hardly likely to make a break for it.

The guards waited inattentively by the cart as the last of the parcels were taken into the office. No one paid any attention to Linck and Flynn who were leaning casually against a wall a few feet from the parcels office. It was, after all, the prisoners' court-

The Adolf Hitler Bridge spanning the river Mulde, on the route to the Castle, from the station. The picture shows the arrival of the Belgian contingent in July 1943.

yard.

One of the orderlies picked up the last bag and disappeared into the office. So did Linck and Flynn. As two British prisoners engaged the guards in a diversionary conversation, Linck and Flynn were wriggling their way into two large bags held open by the Polish orderlies in the corridor to the parcels office. Within seconds, the necks of the bags were securely tied and carried out to the cart where the guards were still involved in a meaningless conversation.

Linck and Flynn were in the cart – but in more senses than one. Before the orderlies had time to inform the guards they were ready to go, four rifle-wielding soldiers, led by a senior officer, suddenly appeared from across the courtyard, climbed on to the back of the cart and began viciously kicking the bags. Cries of pain soon confirmed what the Germans had clearly known. Linck, Flynn and the two Poles were unceremoniously marched away. They each received three weeks' solitary confinement.

That van den Heuvel's plan was thwarted by the actions of a collaborator was never conclusively proved, but he and Linck believed it too much of a coincidence that the Germans should suddenly spot-check the bags on that particular day and appear to know exactly what they were looking for. The Poles had their suspicions, too. A few weeks later, the Senior Polish Officer, Gen. Tadeusz Piskor, went to the Kommandant, Col. Schmidt, to inform him that he had uncovered an informer. He had been tried before a court of fellow officers and it was, added the General, the unanimous verdict that he should be hanged. The traitor was transferred from Colditz Castle later that day.

A similar escape plan had been attempted by the British some months earlier on 5 August, 1941. It involved Peter Allan and John Hyde-Thompson.

It was literally a spur-of-the-moment plan by the British Escape Officer, Pat Reid, following a sudden visit by French prisoners who had been assigned the task of carrying palliasses from an attic store above the British quarters to a waiting cart in the prisoners' courtyard. Ironically, they were being removed as part of a security clamp-down to dcny the inventive prisoners potential escape material.

Allan, because of his slight build, was selected

The post cart, used by Linck and Flynn in their escape attempt, standing in the yard of the Kommandantur.

to make the attempt, which depended entirely upon French co-operation, for it was Reid's plan that the Frenchmen should dump Allan on to the cart hidden inside a palliasse.

The palliasses were to be taken to a store in the town. Allan would have little trouble in breaking out when the coast was clear. He spoke excellent German and had the required degree of determination and nerve. All in all, if the French co-operated, he had every chance of getting to the comparative safety of Poland.

While he was being rigged out in civilian clothing and given the necessary forged documents and German money from the prisoners' 'escape store', Reid was busy persuading a reluctant French soldier to carry Allan to the cart.

The plan had worked like a dream. The cart, packed high with palliasses, was unloaded at the store room in town. The German guards had seen nothing. Allan cut himself free and found himself on the first floor of an unoccupied house. He climbed out of a rear window, dropped down into a garden and began his gruelling cross-country journey to Poland.

Later that afternoon, the British were ready to make another attempt. Hyde-Thompson was selected because of his generous contribution to the prisoners' escape fund of illicitly acquired Reichsmarks. But he was not the wisest choice because he was tall and heavy. The French had trouble lifting him on to the cart. They panicked, leaving him on the ground at the rear of the cart. Vital minutes passed. A German NCO, who was supervising the transport, accidentally stepped back into the palliasse. Its hardness puzzled him.

The palliasse was cut open to reveal a straw-covered Hyde-Thompson. An immediate roll call was announced. Allan was missing. A German patrol raced to the house where the palliasses had been dumped earlier in the day. There they discovered the torn palliasse and an open window. Hyde-Thompson was later sentenced to one month's solitary confinement.

Allan succeeded in getting out of Germany, but was finally recaptured in Vienna after his pleas for help were rejected by officials at the American Consulate. The Americans, in a delicate state of neutrality, could not be sure that Allan was not an espionage agent planted by the Germans. Allan simply failed to convince them. He slept rough in the Austrian capital until, exhausted mentally and phy-

sically, he wandered in desperation into a local hospital. The German authorities were informed of the arrival of the dishevelled and desolate stranger. Within days, Allan, who had travelled so far and so valiantly, was back in Colditz Castle.

Opposite page: 2nd Lt. Peter Allan, who spoke fluent German, complete with escape outfit.
Below: A bag of parcels destined for another camp.

Bottom: A caricature of Cameron Highlander Peter Allan's escape drawn by French Capt. Moizenko. Capt. Paul Priem, the Senior Security Officer, who was known to be fond of the bottle, is bemoaning the fact that his Castle isn't a fortress and the Scots come and fly out as they please.

CHAPTER 6

DUPED - BY THE DUTCH DUMMIES

THERE WERE TWO silent witnesses to the great manhole escape plan. They were privy to a most damning conspiratorial conversation that any German Security Officer would have given a month's pay to have eavesdropped on. But the two mute figures posed no threat. While they resembled Dutch officers, they were no more than skilfully-constructed dummies, but the part they were to play was vital to the Dutch plan. And the Dutch, as their escape tactics illustrated time and again, were remarkably ingenious. Their flamboyant inventiveness bordered almost on impertinence. The dummies, Max and Moritz, were to come into play in the final stage of a plan which centred on the Castle park, visited daily by the prisoners for recreation.

The Kommandant, Col. Schmidt, and his Senior Security Officers knew the park was the weak spot in their fortifications. But the High Command in Berlin insisted the prisoners should have fresh air every day, in accordance with a Geneva Convention ruling. The trouble was that less than half of the 700 prisoners were ever interested in the daily two-hour recreational period, yet the security arrangements had to be as elaborate as those necessary to safeguard the entire Castle for twenty-four hours. In 1941 the Dutch were to prove that Schmidt had good reason for believing the park a serious security risk.

They were to exploit it in broad daylight under the noses of ten soldiers, an NCO and an officer, assigned to guard them. Ironically, the first stage of the escape route was inadvertently provided by the Kommandant's own Security Officers who had marked off an area in the Castle park for a football pitch. Near one of the touchlines, the Dutch discovered a manhole cover, three feet square, which was the inspiration for their brilliantly inventive Escape Officer, Capt. Machiel van den Heuvel.

But first he had to establish its depth, so for several days a number of his officers sat in a group around the manhole cover while one of them read, with an apparent air of piety, uplifting passages from the Bible. Their thoughts, in fact, were concentrated on nothing more uplifting than the removal of the manhole cover. Once the guards had become accustomed to this godly scene, one of the Dutchmen produced a spanner skilfully made out of parts of the prisoners' iron beds. He slotted the jaws of the spanner round the head of the large bolt at the centre of the cover and, placing a heel against its handle, pushed gently at first until under increasing pressure the bolt began to turn. A few moments later, it had been removed.

While the attention of the nearby guards was distracted by a football match, the cover was lifted. They saw a water conduit at a depth of about eight feet. There was ample room in which to conceal two men. The cover, and the huge bolt, which had a thread of three-quarters of an inch in diameter, were replaced. Van den Heuvel and his colleagues were well pleased with the day's work. The Bible group members continued their studies, happy in the knowledge that the Lord was looking after his children.

Van den Heuvel had already solved a major problem, which was how two men could be hidden in the manhole yet not be missed when the prisoners were checked before their return to the Castle. They were counted at the Castle departure point, and on their arrival at the entrance to a recreational compound, to make sure none had disappeared en route, then again at the end of the period. It later became a practice even to stop the men for random checks on their way back to the Castle. Finally, on their arrival, they would be counted once more. Kommandant Schmidt wanted the prisoners to know that they were watched every step of the way.

If the Dutch escapers were to have a reasonable chance of putting a good distance between themselves and Colditz, it was also important to conceal their absence from the first evening roll call.

For all of this, van den Heuvel had hit upon a simple ruse. The number of prisoners arriving at the Castle by the late summer of 1941 was growing rapidly, and the roll call, held four times a day, was a tedious task for the soldiers. The sooner it was over the better. They didn't stop to study facial detail. Van den Heuvel reasoned that two expressionless figures, staring straight ahead, would attract the attention of a soldier for no longer than it would take to count them. Enter Max and Moritz.

To construct the dummies' heads, the Dutch recruited the ready help of a Polish officer who was an accomplished amateur sculptor.

It was decided that the heads would be made of plaster, which could be obtained without difficulty from a civilian builder, nicknamed 'Slam', who frequently visited the Castle to carry out repairs and was known for his willingness to accept a bribe. Its comparative lightness would make the dummies easier to carry.

The Pole had to make several attempts before he was able to master the difficulty of moulding the quick-hardening plaster. But, finally, the heads were perfect in every detail. Painting them was the next task and that was done by a Royal Dutch Naval Lieutenant, Baron Diederick van Lynden, who later

Inset: Lt. Leo de Hartog holding 'Moritz'. Left to right: Dutch officers Lt. Frits Kruimink, Lt. Diederick van Lynden, Gijs van Nimwegen, 'Moritz', Lt. Leo de Hartog, Lt. Herman Donkers, Lt. Down van den Krapp, Major Coen Giebel.

was to become the Dutch Ambassador to West Germany. The paint and pastels were obtained from Lt. John Watton, of the Border Regiment, who held art classes for the prisoners. Two weeks later, van Lynden had finished. The heads were fixed to makeshift frames, Army long coats draped around them, and officers' hats placed upon their heads. Van den Heuvel inspected the dummies from every angle. He was sure they were good enough to fool the Germans.

The officers chosen to baptise van den Heuvel's plan in the autumn of 1941 were Lt. Hans Larive and Lt. Franz Steinmetz, of the Royal Netherlands Navy.

It began with a group of Dutch officers, some of them wearing army great coats and others long black cloaks, arriving at the iron trellis gate entrance to the prisoners' courtyard, which was the assembly point for prisoners wishing to take daily exercise. Prisoners of various nationalities stood around in disorderly fashion while they were counted.

The number was duly recorded, but it did not include Larive and Steinmetz who were out of sight, crouching under the long black cloaks worn by two of their taller countrymen. The cloaks, part of the Polish officers' uniform and loaned to the Dutch for the occasion, came well below the knees, giving excellent cover. The two tall Dutchmen were at the centre of the large group, making it impossible for the soldiers to notice two extra pairs of feet.

The prisoners never walked to the park in organised file. It was their practice to amble in groups or singly and at varying pace, their defiance of regimentation all part of the psychological battle against German authority. So nothing appeared unusual when the group moved slowly to make it as

easy as possible for Larive and Steinmetz, their bodies bent uncomfortably low in crouching positions.

Once in the park, the Dutch made their way to the football pitch and the manhole cover. Larive and Steinmetz, on a pre-arranged signal, darted out from under the cloaks to join their colleagues in the Bible study lesson. The plan, so far, was working perfectly. The Dutch waited several minutes to give the guards time to settle into their regular pattern, to relax their vigilance, watching the prisoners doing their damn stupid exercises or sitting around in idle conversation.

Finally, Lt. Cdr. Damiaan van Doorninck, Royal Dutch Navy, the leader of the phoney Bible study group gave a signal to the officer who had hidden the home-made spanner. Sitting almost on top of the manhole cover, he moved cautiously,

keeping his movements to an absolute minimum to avoid attracting attention.

As at the first attempt, the thick bolt was removed within minutes. Van Doorninck looked round to make sure the guards had noticed nothing to arouse their suspicions before he gave the final signal. In one rapid movement, two officers removed the cover and in a matter of seconds Larive and Steinmetz were inside the manhole and the cover was replaced. The Bible study continued in a joyous air of love and spiritual harmony. The two-hour recreational period came to an end. The prisoners assembled at the compound gate, were

Below: The Dutch contingent. Front row centre, Major E. Engles, Royal Netherlands Indies Army; Front row far right, Lt. Cdr. Damiaan J. van Doorninck, Royal Netherlands Navy.

counted and returned to the castle.

Shortly before roll call that evening, the Dutch held a final rehearsal in their quarters and when the time came to assemble in the prisoners' courtyard, they moved off for the final act in the escape drama. The dummies' heads and their hoop-shaped torsos were hidden under long cloaks and carried by Cadet Officers Leo de Hartog and Willem Grizjen, both young and strong enough for the muscle-straining task ahead.

In an exaggerated mêlée of forming rank and file, and surrounded by their colleagues, de Hartog and Grizjen quickly assembled the dummies. Two pairs of army boots were produced and placed beneath the cloaks to complete the illusion. The routine of roll call normally took about thirty minutes, barring time-wasting tactics.

The soldier assigned to the Dutch contingent counted at an unhurried rate, stabbing the air with a forefinger in the direction of each man. De Hartog and Grizjen were at the centre of the middle rank to put the maximum distance on all sides between them and the German. The strain of holding the dummies alongside them was as great as the temptation to sneak a glance at the guard to see if there was any reaction. But, as instructed by van den Heuvel, they stood ramrod stiff, staring straight ahead.

The soldier made no sudden movement, gave no shout of alarm. After what must have seemed like an eternity to the two Dutchmen, he moved on to count the rank behind them and finally they were dismissed. The Dutch were ecstatic as they made their way back to their quarters, knowing the success of their ruse would gain Larive and Steinmetz vital time on the first leg of their long journey to the safety of Switzerland.

Their emergence that night from the manhole was a comparatively safe and simple affair: safe because the park was well away from the Castle walls so not patrolled, simple, due to the further ingenuity of van den Heuvel.

After the prisoners left the recreational compound, the area was always searched for any signs of escape activity. It was, therefore, vital for the manhole cover to appear to have been undisturbed with the bolt firmly in place. The Dutch solution was to have a glass tubing bolt made, identical to the real one, with a wooden head painted the same colour as the genuine bolt.

When they were ready to break out, Larive and Steinmetz pushed against the cover, shattering the glass tubing. After climbing out, they cleared up the

broken glass and, with the home-made spanner, screwed down the cover with the real bolt which had been given to them seconds before they had jumped into the manhole.

They got safely to Switzerland after travelling via Tuttlingen in south-west Germany. They were the first Dutch officers to debunk the escape-proof reputation of Colditz Castle.

The Germans suspected the escape had some connection with the park area, but could find no clues. Kommandant Schmidt renewed his argument with the High Command about stopping recreation periods in the interest of security, but Berlin continued to insist on adherence to the Geneva Convention, for which they were rewarded by two further two-man escapes over a matter of weeks, one of which was successful. Four out of six – it was an amazing record.

The manhole ruse was eventually discovered at its most vulnerable point – when the escapers had to disappear down into the hole. More guards had been assigned to the park by the desperate Kommandant and eventually Lt. Geoff 'Stooge' Wardle and the Pole, Lt. Wojchieckowski, were caught in the act. The result was twenty-one days solitary for them and metal clamps to reinforce the manhole cover bolt.

The dummies, however, were still undiscovered and very much in active service, and the audacity of the Dutch was demonstrated by another attempt from the park a few weeks later. They were relying on the Germans not expecting another escape so soon from the same area. The plan had the Dutch stamp of flair, imagination and daring. In fact it was to prove a touch too daring. It meant the Germans would be given the chance of seeing the dummies for the first time close to and in broad daylight, instead of in the fading light of evening roll call at some distance.

Even though the authorities had not worked out how the manhole escapers reached the park undetected, they had unwittingly been thinking along the right lines when prisoners were instructed to carry their great coats and cloaks over their arms on the way to and from the park. This meant that with nothing to hide under would-be park escapers had to reckon with being seen and counted on the

Right: Dutch officers in the prisoners' yard. Capt. Machiel van den Heuvel is third from left in the back row. Above right: The camouflaged canvas.

they were being exceptionally disorderly. His interest was suddenly taken by an officer in the midst of the Dutch. He stepped forward and ordered the men to his left and right to move apart, and a moment later, it was all over. The first of the dummies had been discovered.

A rapid count was made and it didn't take the Alsatians long to sniff out the two Dutch officers, Lt. Frits Kruimink and Capt. Down van den Krapp, hiding in the recreational compound under a large section of canvas to which hundreds of leaves had been painstakingly sewn.

Astonishingly, the Germans failed to conclude that as two men had attempted to escape there must have been another dummy officer among the prisoners to make up the number. In the alarm and

Previous page: A roll call in summer wasn't too much of a hardship.
Right: Roll call, Christmas 1942, the Poles in the foreground. Above: Roll call in winter was a different story.

way from the Castle. The dummies, therefore, had to go into action earlier in the plan.

It was now mid-December, a cold, windy day, and when the sharp whistle blast signalled the end of the recreation in the park, the prisoners gathered together for the head count before returning to the Castle. There was a larger than usual turn out for that exercise period, and this had already triggered off an alarm bell inside the head of Hauptmann Paul Priem. It didn't make sense, particularly on such a wretchedly cold day.

His suspicions were aroused even further by the actions of the prisoners. They were never exactly obedient or co-operative, anything to annoy or disrupt. But now, as the head count was taking place, confusion that followed the discovery of the dummy being carried by de Hartog, Willem Grizjen's dummy was quickly dismantled and hidden under an army great coat. Later, another head was made in readiness for another escape plan. But the dummies were discovered accidentally in a security search two months later – in February 1942 – by the No. 1 Security Officer, Reinhold Eggers.

Capt. Machiel van den Heuvel and his colleagues were transferred from Colditz Castle on 7 June, 1943, to a prisoner-of-war camp at Stanislav in south-east Poland. On 4 January, 1944, they were again transferred, this time to Neubrandenburg, north of Berlin, from where they were liberated by the Russians on 28 April, 1945.

Van den Heuvel died in Java on 24 June, 1947, while fighting the Indonesians in their battle for independence. Cadet Officer Leo de Hartog, who, with Cadet Officer Willem Grizjen, was responsible for carrying the dummies, continued his military career on his return to Holland on 1 June, 1945, finally retiring in May 1973, as Colonel of a tank regiment, the Royal Hussars of Prince Alexander.

De Hartog later said: 'The manhole plan was quite fantastic. It was a brilliant idea by Capt. van den Heuvel. In a way, he was a genius. He was also a very brave man, a truly professional soldier whose death was a sad loss. I think, if he had lived, he would have risen to much greater rank. When he died he was in the thick of the action, leading his men with great courage.'

CHAPTER 7

ESCAPE EQUIPMENT

PRÄSIDENT IN BERLIN.
Abteilung II.
AUSLÄNDERAMT.

BERLIN, den 10. Januar 1945.

PASSERSATZ (gültig bis 10. Juli 1945)

Der Polizeipräsident in Berlin bescheinigt hiermit – nach eingezogener Erkundigung bei der kgl. schwedischen Gesandtschaft – dass PIETER BERG, geboren am 2. Mai 1909 in Ede, die niederländische Staatsangehörigkeit besitzt.

Herr Berg steht als ständiger Reisender im Dienste der Firma Max Lindner, Maschinenbau, Berlin.

Seine Aufgabe ist, die von seiner Firma gelieferten Maschinen, – deren Bezahlung noch nicht stattgefunden hat – zu kontrollieren.

Dazu ist ihm eine allgemeine Reiseerlaubnis für das Reichsgebiet erteilt worden.

Da Herr Berg durch Bombenterror seine Besitzungen verloren hat, gilt diese Bescheinigung als Passersatz bis zum 10. Juli 1945.

Der Polizeipräsident in Berlin.
I.A.

Unterschrift des Inhabers:

Unterschrift des Arbeitgebers:

Gebührenfrei

Reiseerlaubnis

Strecke

Gültig bis 10 Juli 1945

Berlin 10 Januar 1945

Der Polizeipräsident in Berlin
I.A.

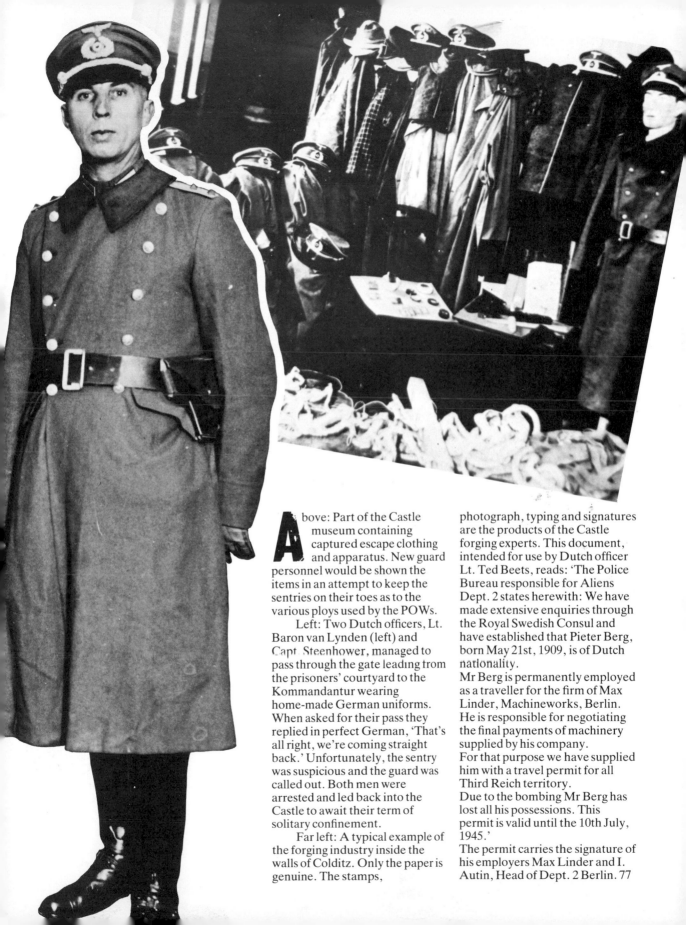

Above: Part of the Castle museum containing captured escape clothing and apparatus. New guard personnel would be shown the items in an attempt to keep the sentries on their toes as to the various ploys used by the POWs.

Left: Two Dutch officers, Lt. Baron van Lynden (left) and Capt. Steenhower, managed to pass through the gate leading from the prisoners' courtyard to the Kommandantur wearing home-made German uniforms. When asked for their pass they replied in perfect German, 'That's all right, we're coming straight back.' Unfortunately, the sentry was suspicious and the guard was called out. Both men were arrested and led back into the Castle to await their term of solitary confinement.

Far left: A typical example of the forging industry inside the walls of Colditz. Only the paper is genuine. The stamps, photograph, typing and signatures are the products of the Castle forging experts. This document, intended for use by Dutch officer Lt. Ted Beets, reads: 'The Police Bureau responsible for Aliens Dept. 2 states herewith: We have made extensive enquiries through the Royal Swedish Consul and have established that Pieter Berg, born May 21st, 1909, is of Dutch nationality.

Mr Berg is permanently employed as a traveller for the firm of Max Linder, Machineworks, Berlin. He is responsible for negotiating the final payments of machinery supplied by his company.

For that purpose we have supplied him with a travel permit for all Third Reich territory.

Due to the bombing Mr Berg has lost all his possessions. This permit is valid until the 10th July, 1945.'

The permit carries the signature of his employers Max Linder and I. Autin, Head of Dept. 2 Berlin. 77

THE DEGREE OF INVENTIVENESS and ingenuity achieved by Colditz prisoners in the manufacture of tools and apparatus, and their craftsmanship in the subsequent production of forged documents, bogus German uniforms, civilian clothing and general escape aid requirements is, even by today's standards, truly astonishing.

Their achievements included a typewriter, a sewing machine, a camera, compasses, complex keys to break high security locks and imitation stamps of authorisation. From stolen lead piping and 78 r.p.m. records, melted and poured into clay moulds, came buttons for the bogus uniforms and civilian clothing; from cardboard, linoleum, art-class paint and black boot polish came swastika and ornate eagle-wing badges, leggings, belts and gun holsters; floorboards provided the wood for skilfully carved imitation rifles and stars denoting officer rank; stripped electrical wiring supplied the piping for officers' hats and forage caps.

The uniforms were tailored from the prisoners' own uniforms. The results, as the photographs in this book illustrate, were remarkable. They had to be. The success of an escape was the ultimate tribute to the many and varied skills of the back-room boys who worked so tirelessly for the benefit of their

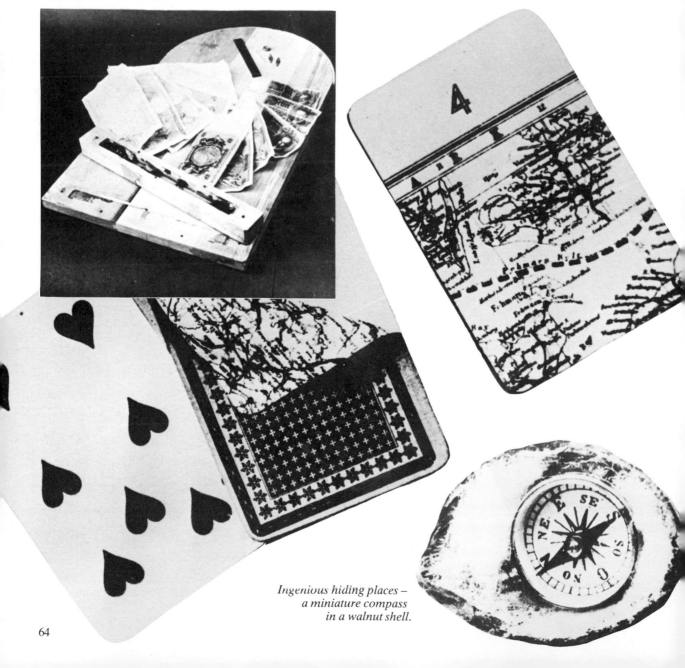

Ingenious hiding places –
a miniature compass
in a walnut shell.

colleagues.

Their accomplishments were all the more incredible when one considers they were achieved with home-made tools, constructed ingeniously of scrap metal and material stolen or obtained through bribery. Wood planes, drills, saws and hammers were made in this fashion and the results prisoners achieved with these make-shift tools stun belief.

The typewriter, for example, not only operated efficiently, but its typeface resembled perfectly that found on official documents. It was made by a Polish officer, Lt. Niedenthal, who carved the letters out of wood. The machine was mostly made of wood and could be rapidly dismantled in the event of a sudden raid. The typewriter ribbon was acquired through bribery. Unfortunately, I was not able to obtain a photograph of the machine, but its results are shown in a photograph of a forged document.

The camera was also a marvellous example of craftsmanship and ingenuity. It was used to supply photographs for forged work permits, although a 'souvenir' photograph was taken with it of Dick Howe, who is pictured with a miniature radio smuggled in components into the Castle. The film and processing paper, items the prisoners certainly couldn't manufacture, were the results of a bribe.

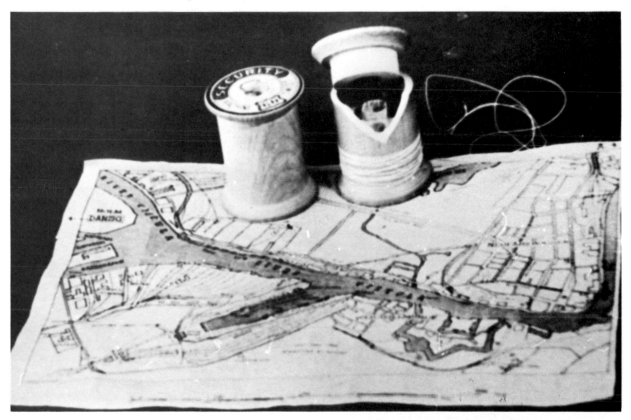

Opposite page, far left: A simple game of shove halfpenny contains escape money, map and compasses. The black rubber strip at the top of the board, used to shove the coins, contains a saw.
Opposite page: A pack of playing cards conceal numbered map sections which, when placed together, reveal a composite map of German occupied territories, showing possible escape routes. Above: Cotton reels make good hiding places for maps. Right: Hidden compartment in coat hangers.

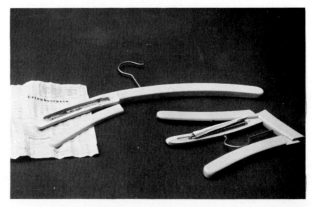

Most of the forged paperwork had to be done by hand and in gothic German script. It was a tedious task that demanded concentration and infinite care. The slightest slip would destroy days of effort. The nibs, obtained from the canteen for legitimate letter writing, were filed down to an angle to give a broad and narrow script. Finer detail was usually completed by the use of a single hair of an artist's brush. Lt. Herman Donkers, of the Royal Netherlands Indies Army, became an accomplished forger and his eyesight was eventually irreparably damaged through the strain, a fate shared by other camp forgers as well. The results of their efforts are startling for their apparent authenticity and require expert examination to discern the fake. The same standard was achieved in the production of stamps of authorisation cut out of linoleum. Some excellent examples are illustrated in the photograph of a fake travel permit in the name of Pieter Berg, alias Lt. Ted Beets, a Dutch officer, who planned to attempt to escape from Colditz in January 1945. In the event it was never used. The photograph shows the fake stamp of a police administrative department giving him authority to travel and explains that his identity papers were lost in a bombing raid.

The skill and time required to make an imita-

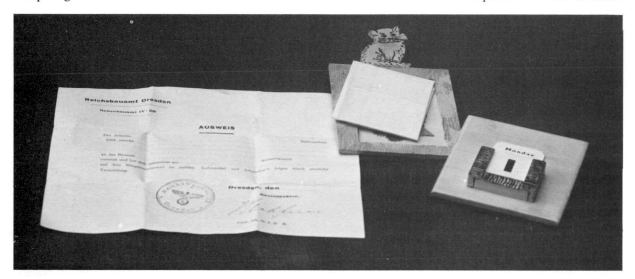

tion stamp were considerable. For that reason, the Dutch were shattered when, in January 1943, a search by the Security staff discovered a cache of escape material hidden under the floorboards of their quarters. The hoard included three hundred Reichsmarks, smuggled into the Castle to finance overland journeys, and more than a dozen highly treasured fake stamps of varying 'authority', including police departments and the Oberkommando der Wehrmacht, the High Command in Berlin.

The search party also found the equipment that lock-picking expert, Cdr. Damiaan van Doorninck, Dutch Navy, used to measure the mechanism of the Castle's complex Zeiss Ikon or cruciform locks. The key is most simply described as a four-sided Yale key, each side of a different design. Van Doorninck's equipment, which was made out of scrap metal, included a gauge to measure the drop of the lock's pistons. However, by 1943 its capture was not a disaster, as there were enough keys in circulation, cut and forged out of bucket handles, for copies to be made if and when necessary.

The prisoners' mastery in picking locks sorely tried the Security hierarchy. Time and again they found rooms they believed to be safely locked were being gradually stripped of all potential escape

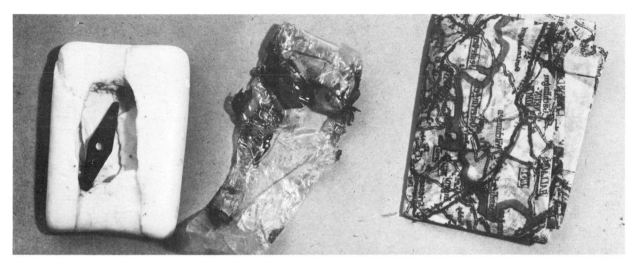

Opposite page: Hidden compartment in a calendar. Left: A draughts board containing forged identity cards, from a 'games parcel', sent from Harrods and draughts set containing tablets.
Above: Escape map, sweets in cellophane and a compass hidden in a bar of soap, the minimum requirements for an escaping POW.
Opposite page: a wooden sewing machine, the inspiration of Lt. John Hamilton-Baillie, Royal Engineers. Primarily designed as a chain stitch machine it was later re-designed for lock stitch. Neither model proved satisfactory and both kept dropping stitches. It was officially put to use on stage costumes and scenery. Also a lathe made by Flt. Lts. Bill Goldfinch and Jack Best, from gramophone engines and scrap metal. It was useful in making dummy rifle bolts, barrels and keys. Below: Stamps cut from linoleum.

material. That is why the Zeiss Ikon locks were installed, but once the prisoners worked out their mechanism, burglary continued unabated. Each nation had its own lock-picking maestro. Lt. W. L. B. 'Scarlet' O'Hara of the Royal Tank Regiment was the British expert, while Lt. Gigue and Lt. Surmanowicz filled the office for the French and the Poles.

Basic escape equipment such as a compass was child's play to make; by repeatedly stroking the points of two needles with a fixed pole magnet. They would be pushed horizontally through both sides of the apex of a press-stud to balance each other and then balanced on another needle for free movement.

The dyeing of bogus uniforms and civilian clothing was also a comparatively easy affair. Dye came from a variety of sources, including coloured crepe paper, which the Germans allowed in unlimited quantity for making costumes for stage productions in the prisoners' theatre. Another source was the indelible lead of pencils obtained from the canteen which would be finely ground down and used as an additive in dyeing trousers to the correct battledress shade.

The task of making identical German uniforms

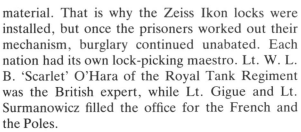

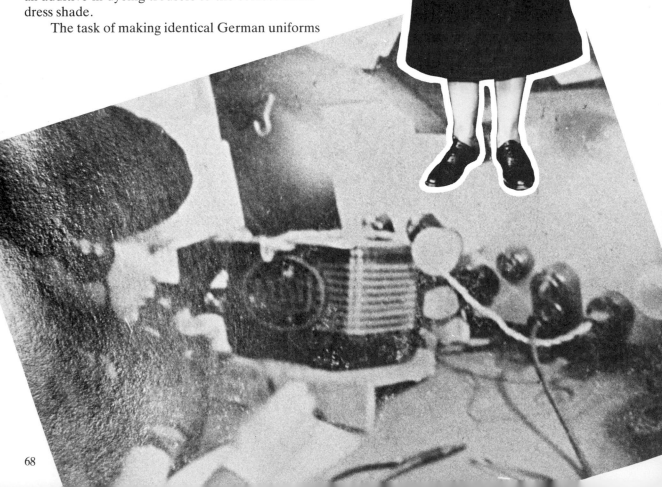

Left: Capt. Dick Howe, Royal Tank Regiment, Escape Officer 1942–5, operating the illicit wireless. Top right are the 'stooging lights' which would flash to warn of danger. The radio, which was for receiving not transmitting, had been smuggled into Colditz in parts. Sadly for the British it was discovered in 1944.

Above left: French Lt. Bouley spent months preparing this escape gear. The wig was sent him by his wife. He wore an overcoat over his disguise as he walked down to the park for exercise. Then, on reaching a blind corner along the path, his comrades whipped away the coat, he placed the wig and hat on his head, made an about face, and began walking back along the path. All went well until he dropped his watch and an English officer, not realising who he was, picked it up and gave it to the guard, telling him 'the lady' had dropped it. The guard took off in pursuit. Lt. Bouley heard the guard approach, assumed he had been spotted, and gave up the attempt.

Above: Prisoners requiring prolonged hospitalisation or specialised treatment would be transferred from Colditz to the nearest hospital capable of dealing with their particular malady. A journey outside the Castle walls presented a heaven-sent opportunity for escape and, with this in mind, prisoners would cultivate suitable symptoms with the help of privately acquired medical supplies which could be authorised at the request of a medically qualified colleague. Others managed to fool the doctors without the use of drugs, using self-hypnosis, will-power or yoga.

German censors discovered a message concealed in a parcel of medical supplies, addressed to French Capt. Arditti. With the message were a fake permit, instructions on his escape route and details regarding his new identity.

Security kept an eye open for further developments and soon another parcel arrived for the French officer and among the items enclosed, they found a hair brush containing three ampoules and a signed medical note stating that Arditti had suffered from gall bladder trouble since his sixteenth birthday.

Captain Arditti's visit to the hospital was cancelled . . .

took on factory-line efficiency with the construction of a sewing machine by Lt. John Hamilton-Baillie of the Royal Engineers. The German authorities had permitted him to make it for the manufacture of stage costumes.

While the production of escape equipment, clothing and documents verged at times on a cottage industry, the flow of contraband into Colditz Castle to aid escapes was no small affair. It came from families, relatives and friends and, because they were so cunningly concealed, presented a serious challenge to the Security staff.

The photographs show some of the ingenious hiding places: a compass hidden in a walnut; numbered map sections attached to the backs of playing cards; forged identity cards hidden in a draughts board which, according to the label, was purchased at Harrods.

Also revealed are some of the prisoners' hiding places for their forged escape documents. They included a calendar stand, coat hangers, a shaving mirror and a bar of soap, which contained a compass and cellophane-wrapped sweets as escape rations.

In his book, *Colditz – the German Viewpoint*, Reinhold Eggers records intercepting a secret letter to a French officer, Capt. Arditti, enclosing some false travel papers, along with the following advice:

> Don't talk too much while you are travelling. Remember you have worked in Coswig, near Dresden, and that you live at Dijon, 12 Rue de la Gare. If you are travelling home on these papers, don't stop in Paris. There are always sudden searches in the streets and it is the most dangerous place in the whole of occupied France. Keep to the line Riesa-Leipzig-Erfurt-Kassel-Cologne-Liége. I take it you have all the civvies you need.

Arditti later received another parcel whose contents were microscopically examined. It contained, among other items, a hair brush which, as the photograph shows, had a false top which concealed three ampoules plus a pre-dated medical letter stating that Arditti had suffered from a gall bladder ailment since he was sixteen years old. The ampoules contained a drug to simulate the appropriate symptoms, which would have almost certainly got Arditti into a local hospital from where, in a moment of lax supervision, he would have undoubtedly attempted to escape. Needless to say, he didn't get to hospital.

THE DAY THE GERMANS SAW DOUBLE

CHAPTER 8

French Lt. André Perodeau, left, Willy Pöhnert, right.

THERE WERE MANY physical similarities between the thirty-two-year-old Frenchman, Lt. André Perodeau, of the 62nd Regiment of Infantry, and Herr Willy Pöhnert, a civilian electrician whose job it was to maintain electrical installations and equipment in Colditz Castle. They were similar in height, weight, colouring, facial bone structure and age.

Lt. Perodeau had seen the slightly built German labourer on a number of occasions when, tool bag in hand, he ambled around from job to job in the prisoners' quarters accompanied by a soldier.

He studied him carefully. There was, without doubt, a remarkable likeness. The question was: could he, in labourer's clothes identical to those Willy always wore and with the necessary forged documents, deceive the sentries at the Castle's security posts and simply walk to freedom by impersonating the affable electrician?

The Frenchman had the nerve required to carry out such a plan. Only five months earlier, he had successfully escaped from Oflag 4D by switching roles with a trusted French orderly whose duties included the collection of rubbish. With a fellow countryman, he had calmly walked out of the prisoner-of-war camp carrying containers of rubbish.

Unfortunately, the alarm was sounded before they could travel fifty kilometres and they were recaptured three hours later by a German patrol. As a result, the Breton Lieutenant was transferred, in July 1941, to the maximum security of Colditz Castle.

His decision made, and his plan approved by his superior officer, Gen. Emil le Brigant, Perodeau began to observe Willy Pöhnert at every possible opportunity. The precise colour and style of his work clothes were carefully noted. They included Willy's flat cap and a red woollen scarf which he wore cravat-style and without which he was rarely seen. Then there were his mannerisms – was there anything distinctive about his style of walking? Did he tend to walk quickly or slowly? Did he slouch or hold his shoulders smartly back? Upon such precise observation could very well rest Perodeau's success or failure at the four security posts within the Castle.

The time was late November 1941. The plan would be put into operation shortly before Christmas Day when the vigilance of the guards would not be so keen, as they fortified themselves over a glass or more of festive schnapps. There was much to be done in those four weeks. It was necessary to 'tailor' labourer's clothing identical to that worn by Willy and also manufacture the civilian clothes which Perodeau would wear underneath his labourer's garb for his journey across Germany to Switzerland.

There was also one other item, the most important of all – a forgery of the identity pass which permitted Willy unrestricted access to the Castle. This turned out to be an almost insurmountable problem. To attempt to acquire Willy's pass, through fair means or foul, was to court disaster. As a possible ally, he was an unknown quantity. Although he appeared friendly enough, none of the French prisoners had had the opportunity to test his vulnerability to a bribe. To steal Willy's pass was equally hazardous. The prisoners possessed many illicit talents, but the high degree of pick-pocketing skill required for such a task was not one of them.

There was only one alternative. A situation might arrive in which one of them, for a few fleeting seconds, could study a soldier's pass at fairly close quarters and try his best to commit to memory its overall size, design, colour and stamp details.

The opportunity they had been waiting for presented itself when a French officer, accompanied by a guard, was to go into the town of Colditz to collect Red Cross parcels from the railway station.

After they left the French quarters and passed through the security points at the inner and outer courtyard and at the Castle entrance the officer stood as close as possible to the guard as he produced his identity pass for inspection. On his return, he related to the officer responsible for forged documents all that he could recall about the pass. With that inexact information, the forgery experts went to work.

By now the manufacturing of Willy's work clothes was well under way. The trousers presented little problem. Lt. Edgar Duque, of the 160th Regiment of Artillery, donated his pyjama trousers which were dyed. The cap was fashioned out of a blanket approximately the colour of Willy's cap. A jacket was a more formidable exercise, but in a prison full of creative and imaginative talents, one was soon tailored out of a bed sheet and dyed to the correct colour. A strip of bed sheeting was also used to produce the yellow swastika arm-band. There was one important item left, Willy's conspicuous red woollen scarf, but a Polish officer happened to possess an almost identical one, which he readily tossed into the illegitimate wardrobe of M'sieur Perodeau. As for Willy's glasses, again luck played a hand. Perodeau's own were similar and would be more than adequate to complete the disguise.

The clothes fitted Perodeau well. He paraded around the French quarters in them as fellow officers looked for possible flaws. Maps, Reichsmarks, Red Cross supplies of chocolate, biscuits and figs – enough for two days' travelling – had been packed ready for the moment when Lt. André Perodeau became Willy Pöhnert, civilian electrician. The timing was crucial. Perodeau would have to begin his impersonation at approximately 5.30 p.m., just before the guards changed, so that the delayed Willy, conscientiously repairing an electrical fault caused by a minor act of sabotage in the French quarters, would not encounter the same shift on his own departure.

As Perodeau stepped out from the comparative warmth of the Castle entrance and stood in the darkness of the cobbled courtyard the December night air cut into him, making him grateful for the extra layer he was wearing under his labourer's clothes.

Some twenty yards ahead was the iron trellis gate of the prisoners' courtyard, the first test of his disguise. A single bulb in a lamp socket above the gate cast down a triangle of light upon the sentry.

To Perodeau's relief, the sentry appeared friendly. He gave the pass nothing more than a cursory glance and handed it back. He unlocked the gate and Perodeau walked through.

Then the sentry said something. Perodeau, who spoke hardly a word of German, was prepared for this sort of situation and had perfected right down to the accent, his reply. *'Ich hab's eilig. Ich komme wieder!'* (I am in a hurry. I'll be back later.)

The guard said nothing more, and Perodeau walked numbly on, not quite believing it could be so easy, feeling the eyes of the guard following him, but resisting the temptation to look round.

Just three more security checks.

At the outer courtyard the next sentry stood waiting for him.

Perodeau proffered the pass which was taken without a word. This sentry examined it with officious thoroughness. The seconds passed. The sentry's eyes swivelled upwards to Perodeau, then back to the pass, and Perodeau knew instinctively that he was in trouble. His lack of German meant he had no hope of bluffing his way out. Those few moments seemed eternal. The sentry asked him a question.

Perodeau, unable to reply, could only stand and stare. The sentry repeated the question. Perodeau continued to stare at him dumbly.

Slowly, the sentry lifted the machine gun that hung from his shoulder and pointed the barrel waist-high at Perodeau.

It was all over.

With the machine gun still aimed at Perodeau, the sentry picked up the receiver of the internal telephone to alert the Senior Security Officer on duty. Although there was something clearly wrong with the pass, the sentry was still not absolutely sure that the man standing before him was not Willy Pöhnert the civilian electrician.

He was taken at gun-point back to the first security post. Perodeau realised that it was only a matter of time before the real Willie emerged and his true identity was established. If he could do nothing else, he could put that time to valuable use. The escape kit of maps and German money could be saved for another attempt.

He stood by the gate leading to the prisoners' courtyard, aware that his colleagues, who had observed his capture from their first-floor windows, would be hiding nearby on the other side.

Suddenly, he bent down and pushed the maps and paper money under the gate. By the time his action had registered with the guards and the door was unlocked, the documents and the Frenchmen had disappeared.

Meanwhile the real Willy had moved on from repairing the electrical fault in the French quarters to a job on the third floor, where a search party found him. One of the soldiers said: 'Hey, Willy, what are you doing up here? I've just seen you downstairs.'

Willy, at the end of a long and hard day's work, was not amused. 'Are you crazy?' he replied testily. 'I can't be here and down there at the same time.'

'Come with me then,' said the soldier.

Willy was taken to the office of the Kommandant and was staggered when he saw Perodeau, who was now looking forlorn and down-hearted. To Willy there seemed only one noticeable difference – Perodeau's work clothes were cleaner than his own!

The Castle Kommandant, Col. Schmidt, began firing questions at Willy after informing him that his 'double' standing before him was a French officer who had attempted to escape. Where had he got his clothes from? Had Willy supplied them? Had he taken a bribe to assist the escape?

Repeatedly, the Kommandant fired the same questions at Willy. Repeatedly, the hapless electrician denied all knowledge of the escape plan or any collusion.

Perodeau, not wishing to see Willy suffer unjustly, assured the Kommandant that the confused electrician was totally blameless. The Kommandant finally accepted Willy's pleas of innocence. Suddenly, he laughed, and smiles broke out on the faces of the guards, who had been standing rigidly and sternly to attention.

Turning to Willy, the Kommandant joked: 'It looks as if you have a new-found brother.'

Lt. Perodeau's escape plan had failed because the stamp on his forged pass was glaringly incorrect in a number of major details. As a punishment, he was sentenced to fifteen days in solitary confinement. He never managed to escape from Colditz. When he finally came to leave in July 1943, it was with other French prisoners-of-war to a camp in Lübeck from where he was finally liberated by the British in May 1945.

Of his attempt as Willy's double, he says: 'Those days were exhilarating. Of course I was bitterly disappointed that it failed, not only for myself, but because of all the efforts and unstinting help of my colleagues.'

And Willy's comment? 'The prisoners teased me for weeks. Every time they saw me they would shout: "Hey, here comes M'sieur Perodeau!"'

Left: André Perodeau, Paris 1979. André and Willy became firm friends after the war, and Willy visited the Perodeau family in Paris.

Right: Willy Pöhnert, at his home in the town of Colditz, East Germany, 1978, with a much treasured wall plaque, a gift from the Castle's Polish POWs.

CHAPTER 9
THE CURTAIN RISES

THERE COULD NOT have been a more unlikely setting for an escape attempt than the one that inspired the British to plot a major breakout. For the opening act was planned to take place on the stage of the Castle theatre.

On that stage, where on more legitimate and mundane occasions the prisoners produced plays and shows for their own entertainment, the curtains would rise on a real life drama where there could be no missed cues or muffed lines.

There would, initially, be only two performances and they had to be perfect. The star roles would be played by two British and two Dutch officers, who would operate in teams. If they were successful, other prisoners would follow.

While the conception of the route out of the Castle and its planning was an all-British project, escape liaison between the two nationalities was strong. To the British, Dutchmen who could speak perfect German were invaluable companions for the hazardous journey that would follow through the enemy's homeland. The success of the plan also required nerve, cunning and, as ever, more than a touch of luck. For part of the escape route would take them through the Germans' own quarters. It was a building on the west side of the Castle and adjoining the main gate of the prisoners' courtyard. It accommodated the guard house and the German officers' mess, and through it the escape teams would have nonchalantly to stroll.

The strength of the plan lay in the unashamed impudence. For the Anglo-Dutch escape teams would be suitably dressed in the uniforms of German officers, and indeed were relying heavily on the unquestioning subservience of the German soldier towards his superior officers. The gamble was that none would have the temerity to stop and challenge an officer, particularly in such familiar surroundings. The real risk would come from an officer engaging them in casual conversation.

Once outside the guard house, they would have to pass a sentry on duty near the guard house entrance and two security gates, one under a nearby archway which led to the garrison courtyard and the other under the clock tower which formed an archway leading to a bridge across the long dried-out moat.

At the far end of the bridge was the main gate to the Castle. Positioned there was a final security post which, as the last line in the fortifications, was manned by sentries scrupulous in checking the identification of all departing officers and soldiers.

Left: Airey Neave in the uniform of a German Gefreiter (lance-corporal). The picture was taken in the Kommandant's headquarters after his first attempt to escape through the main gate with a genuine brass security disc obtained by bribery and a bogus message to deliver to the Kommandant from Hauptmann Priem. The tunic and forage cap were of Polish origin and in an attempt to convert their khaki into German field grey, Neave used a mixture of paint from the prisoners' theatricals. He describes what happened next in his book, They Have Their Exits. *The cry of* 'Hände hoch!' *rang out the minute he had passed the first sentry and as he stopped and raised his hands he realised with horror that under the arc lights his paint-daubed uniform and cap* 'shone like a brilliant emerald in the glare. I was a figure of the underworld, a demon king under the spotlights in a Christmas pantomime.'

Camp shows helped pass the time and provided excellent cover for other more secretive and purposeful activities, some starting beneath the stage itself.

The sewing machine was ostensibly in use to create costumes such as these for the camp theatricals. But in quiet corners the backroom boys would also use it to manufacture imitation German uniforms for actors in the real-life drama. Far left: An eloquently patriotic Allied cow steals the scene in this nostalgic Dutch tableau. Left: Stage furniture was built of the minimum materials. Spare wood could serve a much more useful purpose propping a tunnel.

But a chance observation provided a way for the two escape teams to avoid a meticulous examination of their forged identification papers at that final and feared security point.

It was made by Lt. Airey Neave, a twenty-four-year-old officer in the Royal Artillery, who was one of the two British officers selected to take part in the plan. It came about while he was being escorted back from gaol in the town of Colditz after serving twenty-eight days' solitary confinement as a punishment for attempting to escape some four months earlier dressed as a German lance-corporal.

As they began to cross the moat bridge, Neave noticed a wicket gate in the waist-high stone wall which ran the length of the bridge. He also saw that there were steps leading down from the gate to the moat bed, and that further along the moat there were more steps up the steep bank to a pathway which led to married quarters. It was used as a short cut. Just beyond the married quarters lay the Castle park and the route to freedom.

The secret passage which led to the German quarters was discovered by accident. The British Escape Officer, Pat Reid, and a Canadian officer, Flt. Lt. 'Hank' Wardle, of the RAF, had allowed their natural curiosity to take them beneath the roughly constructed stage of the Castle theatre on the top floor of a four-storey building which formed part of the perimeter of the prisoners' courtyard. It was also used to accommodate senior British, Polish, Dutch and French officers.

Beneath the stage, Reid and Wardle, armed

The guard house leading to the prisoners' courtyard. All German personnel had to collect a numbered metal disc from here before entering the prisoners' section which they returned on their way out. It was here that Neave and Perodeau came unstuck. The metal discs can be seen on the wall to the left of the picture.

The security disc belonging to No. 1 Security Officer, Reinhold Eggers.

Kdtr. Oflag IV C
Colditz
Nr. 1

The identity picture which would accompany Lt. Airey Neave to Colditz. It was taken at his first POW camp, Oflag AG IX A Spangenburg.

with home-made saws, cut through the lath and plaster ceiling of a room below. Using a bed-sheet rope tied to a stage support, Reid lowered himself down into the darkness. He found himself in a locked and empty room, which had been long disused. The lock presented no problem and he found himself on an enclosed bridge passing over the main gate of the prisoners' courtyard. On that occasion, Reid went no further, but returned later to resume his intriguing exploration.

On his second visit, he crossed the bridge. The air within the enclosed passage filled his nostrils with a dank, musty odour. The floor was also covered in dust. It was clear that it had not been used for some considerable time. At the far end of the bridge was another locked door, but once through it he immediately realised, for the time being, he could go no further. For he was actually standing in the attic of the guard house. Beyond the attic door was a stone spiral staircase, which led down to the guard house entrance, passing the officers' mess on the first floor and the guard quarters on the ground floor.

Reid's ferreting had indeed produced an escape route that was readily accessible at any time of the day or night and that involved no arduous or time-consuming preparations – the only camouflage required was a white-washed plasterboard to disguise the hole in the ceiling of the room below the stage. If their luck held, it could be used time and again to get dozens of prisoners free of Colditz Castle.

As Escape Officer, it was Reid's prerogative to decide who would make the first attempt and when it would take place. In this case, Reid decided on two attempts to be made on consecutive nights by two-man teams. The British officers selected were Lt. Airey Neave and Lt. John Hyde-Thompson.

The two Dutch officers chosen by Capt. Machiel van den Heuvel were Lt. Toni Luteyn and Lt. Herman Donkers, of the Royal Netherlands Indies Army. They were, in fact, chosen by default. Two other Dutch officers declined the offer, believing that if recaptured their impersonation of German officers would have invalidated their claims to prisoner-of-war status under the Geneva Convention and led to their summary execution. However, Luteyn and Donkers, of more daring spirit, gave little thought to the supposed sanctity of a German officer's uniform and even less to the chances of recapture.

The Dutch supplied the most vital part of the bogus uniforms: pre-war Dutch Home Army great coats which, with slight alterations, were tailored to appear identical to the coats worn by German officers. They were, in fact, blue-green in colour, but in the light of the arc lamps which illuminated the Castle grounds at night, they took on the field grey of the genuine article.

Neave and Luteyn were selected to make the first attempt. Neave decided to take the rank of an Oberleutnant and his forged papers were in the name of Schwartz. Gold stars for the epaulettes to denote his bogus rank were carved from wood and painted by a British colleague. He had good reason to make sure that his uniform this time was correct in every detail. His previous experience, which had resulted in twenty-eight days' solitary confinement, was not lost on the others either.

By the night of 5 January, 1942, everything was ready. Uniforms, documentation, civilian clothes and route maps to Switzerland had all been satisfactorily prepared.

That morning Neave, Luteyn, Reid and Wardle held a final conference. It was agreed that the two men would make their move after nine o'clock evening roll call. The moment the prisoners were

dismissed, the four disappeared inside the theatre building and made their way to the fourth floor. The two bogus uniforms were ready under the stage. Neave and Luteyn changed into them as Reid wrestled with the last lock separating the bridge passage from the guard house attic. For a heart-stopping moment it was recalcitrant, but finally it opened. Reid and Wardle wished them luck and returned the way they had come, locking the doors behind them.

Neave and Luteyn waited several minutes to allow the others to get back into the theatre, replace the plasterboard camouflage and return to their quarters before Luteyn led the way down the stairs.

They could hear organ music wafting up from a wireless in the guards' quarters on the ground floor. The soothing music seemed incongruous. On the first floor a narrow strip of light from the officers' mess spilled out into the dimness of the landing, and they could hear voices within. Thankfully, the door remained closed. They walked stealthily past, and carried on down the steps, breathing a little more easily. Any officer on his way up the staircase would assume they had just left the mess.

Neave and Luteyn walked down the rest of the steps at a more leisurely pace, trying to adopt the swaggering, authoritative air of German officers. In the ground floor passage the door of the guards'

quarters was slightly ajar. Neave caught a glimpse of a German uniform. Maintaining their confident air and unhurried pace, they walked past the guards' quarters and on to the guard house entrance.

Neave hesitated before stepping out into a thick curtain of snow which was falling heavily and spectacularly in the illumination of the arc lights. They knew that just outside the entrance, standing by the main gate to the prisoners' courtyard, was a sentry. He would be their first real test.

Again with all the arrogance he could summon, Neave stepped with theatrical slowness out of the entrance with Luteyn, as a junior officer, closely behind. The sentry, his cap and shoulders covered in

Ballet Nonsense – a full cast on stage. In the orchestra pit, far left, Toni Luteyn; on stage, left, in mortar board and gown, Airey Neave. Neave and Luteyn intended their escape to take place during the finale, believing that the sentries in the guard quarters would take the opportunity to relax their vigil, knowing their Kommandant and his senior officers were guests at the show and out of circulation for a couple of hours.

It also appealed to Neave's sense of humour to disappear beneath the stage – as it were – under their very noses. But delays in their escape preparations resulted in their going at a later date.

snow, ceased stamping his feet the instant he spotted the Oberleutnant. He snapped to attention and gave a smart salute. Neave responded in well-rehearsed fashion.

They walked towards an archway some thirty yards ahead which spanned solitary confinement cells on one side and German soldiers' quarters on the other. At the archway was a security gate, which led to the garrison courtyard.

The sentry opened the gate unhesitatingly, displaying an appropriate degree of deference. Luteyn, with his masterly command of the German language, added a convincing touch to their impersonations by talking to his senior officer about a military matter. Neave, his knowledge of German far from fluent, merely nodded in apparent agreement.

The two officers acknowledged the sentry and continued walking across the garrison courtyard in the direction of the security gate at the clock tower archway, beyond which was the moat bridge.

The snow on that freezing January night was now falling even harder, and an icy, blustery wind caused it to swirl crazily round the courtyard, decreasing visibility to a few yards and giving them ideal cover. None but the insane, they thought, would be forsaking the warmth of their quarters on such a night unless it was absolutely necessary. They were almost at the security gate when they were riveted to the spot by the sight of two figures suddenly emerging out of the snow, walking hurriedly towards them from the direction of the Kommandantur on the far side of the courtyard.

Neave hesitated for a second, believing their absence had been discovered and that the escape plan was about to end in disaster. Instinctively, they kept walking towards the clock tower. The two figures, both under-officers, fell in step behind them. Neave tensed up with fear and tried desperately to relax by putting his hands behind his back, interlocking his gloved fingers. Luteyn, spotting Neave's careless style, quickly checked him. 'Walk with your hands at your side, you bloody fool,' he whispered sharply.

A moment later all four were standing at the security gate waiting for the sentry to let them pass. Luteyn instructed the sentry to open the gate, and they walked out under the clock tower archway. At the wicket gate at the beginning of the moat bridge the under-officers walked past as Luteyn opened the gate for his senior officer.

They took the steps down to the dried-out moat bed as quickly as the blizzard conditions would allow

Above: The escape hatch below stage, with the bed-sheet rope that the four POWs used to climb down into the corridor leading to the guard house.
Right: The POW theatre during a performance. In the front row, second from the left, Reinhold Eggers, Security Officer. On his left Senior British Officer, Lt. Col. W. M. 'Tubby' Broomhall, RE.
Below right: The archway leading from the German quarters. The wicket gate Neave and his comrades used to gain access to the moat is to the right. Part of the Kommandantur can be seen through the archway.

and walked along to the steps leading up to the married quarters.

They were about halfway along the moat bed when a soldier, on his way from the married quarters to the Castle, suddenly appeared out of the darkness. As Neave and Luteyn got near to him, he stopped and stared pointedly at them.

Luteyn, proving again why a German-speaking escape companion was so vital, turned on the soldier. 'Why do you not salute?' he asked angrily. The reprimand, given with all the affronted authority Luteyn could summon, shook the soldier.

He responded by snapping instantly to atten-

tion with a sharp salute. Neave and Luteyn turned away and walked on towards the steps leading out of the moat. In a moment, they were on the pathway to the married quarters. All that separated them from the Castle park wall was the final barrier; a high oak paling fence running along the rear of the married quarters. They scrambled over the palings, stumbling in the snow as they dropped over the other side. They were now in the park and at last out of the far-reaching powerful glare of the Castle's arc lights.

They stumbled for fifty yards, often falling in the snow-covered tangled undergrowth, until they came to the twelve-feet-high stone wall which surrounded the park.

Neave managed to scale the wall with the assistance of Luteyn. He sat astride it to help Luteyn, but the freezing weather was taking its toll of their agility and strength. Time and again, the Dutchman tried without success to maintain his hold of the stones which were covered in snow and ice.

Neave, his fingers numbed of feeling, tried gripping Luteyn's wrists, but balanced precariously on top of the wall, he was unable to support him.

Finally, in a desperate effort, Luteyn managed to climb high enough for Neave to hook his hands under the Dutchman's armpits. Slowly, with Luteyn's feet searching for footholds, Neave was able to hold him long enough for Luteyn to grab the top of the wall and pull himself up.

They were too exhausted from their efforts to talk. They just sat there, astride the wall, their breath puffing cotton wool clouds into the sub-zero night air.

Then Neave, with Luteyn following, jumped from the wall. Their bodies jarred as they landed awkwardly in the darkness. Neave, shaken and with his uniform torn and dishevelled from their stumbling dash through the undergrowth, leaned against a tree. Luteyn sank back against the wall.

They took a minute to recover their energy and their wits. Neave turned to Luteyn. 'Let's go,' he said.

They had beaten Colditz Castle.

Neave and Luteyn, posing as Dutch workers, arrived safely at the Swiss border village of Ramsen on the night of 8 January – just seventy-two hours after their escape from Colditz.

The following morning they were taken to police headquarters in Schaffhausen for security interrogation and then on to their respective legations in Berne.

Neave finally arrived in England in May 1942 after travelling with the help of resistance workers through France and Spain to Gibraltar where he was put on a troopship bound for the Clyde.

Ironically, after the war he was appointed legal liaison officer by the judges at the International Military Tribunal in Nuremberg to serve indictments for war crimes on leading members of Hitler's hierarchy, including Feldmarschall Wilhelm Keitel, Chief of the High Command of the German Armed Forces, Grand Admiral Karl Doenitz, Reichsmarschall Hermann Goering, of the Luftwaffe, and Rudolph Hess, Hitler's deputy.

Neave died tragically on 30 March, 1979, at the hands of IRA terrorists who wired explosives to his car which blew up as he left the House of Commons where for almost twenty-six years he had served as a Conservative Member of Parliament for the constituency of Abingdon, Berkshire. At the time of his death he was Opposition spokesman on Northern Ireland.

Hyde-Thompson and Donkers were also to escape from Colditz Castle the following night of 6 January. But their freedom was short-lived. The absence of Neave and Luteyn from roll call on the morning of the 6th had been concealed through the loan of the

An escaping POW needed forged documents to move around enemy-occupied territory. These are just two of the many produced by amateur forger Lt. Donkers, using the single hair of an artist's brush. The dates would be inserted just prior to his escape.

The Erlaubnisschein *is a forged leave pass, showing the bearer has permission to travel across occupied territory.*

The Bescheinigung *is a certificate showing the bearer has leave-of-absence from his place of work.*

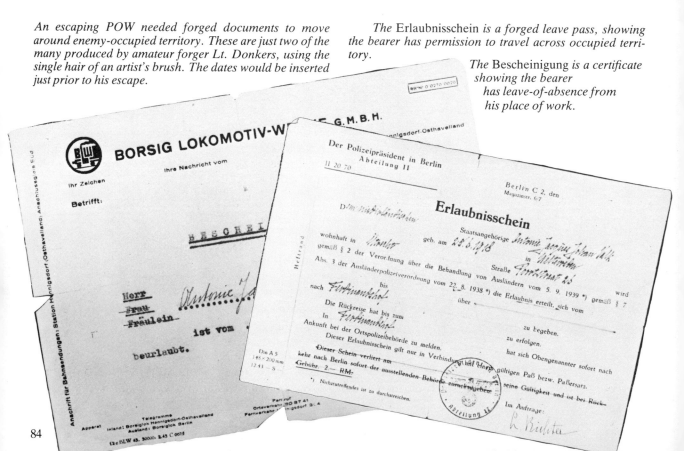

two Dutch dummies to make up the head count. But it was impossible to conceal the additional departure of Hyde-Thompson and Donkers. The Germans duly discovered their absence at roll call the following morning.

By then, however, the two men were well on their way through Germany. They were following the route that Neave and Luteyn had successfully taken. Ironically, it was to lead directly to their recapture.

When Hyde-Thompson and Donkers reached Ulm security had been tightened because of a close shave by Neave and Luteyn only twenty-four hours earlier. A booking office official at the local railway station became suspicious of Neave and Luteyn's work permits when they tried to purchase two tickets to Singen, a town on the Swiss border. Incredibly, a railway policeman, who was alerted by the official, marched them to the State Labour Office and then waited outside while Neave and Luteyn walked unaccompanied into the office. They disappeared out of a rear exit and made a frantic cross-country dash to the neighbouring town of Laupheim, from where they caught a train to Stockach, a village near to the border, and from there completed their journey into Switzerland.

So when the hapless Hyde-Thompson and Donkers, also posing as Dutch workers, arrived at the railway station in Ulm their papers were closely scrutinsed, found to be forgeries and their arrest followed. They were sent back to Colditz Castle to be punished with a term of solitary confinement.

Hyde-Thompson died in Uganda in 1951, just six years after the war ended.

Both Donkers and Luteyn continued service with the Royal Netherlands Indies Army and both attained the rank of Colonel. Donkers retired in 1973 and Luteyn in 1968.

Said Donkers: 'Our escape mission was not really a failure. We learned so much. About ourselves, about the Germans, about the mistakes we made. Above all, we learned to carry on and survive. In the end, man can only be defeated by himself.'

The British were not able to use the theatre escape route again. It was discovered by accident about a week later by a security search team who were looking for the French tunnel described in Chapter 2.

Toni Luteyn, Rijswijk, Holland, 1979

Herman Donkers, Leussen, Holland, 1979.

Lt. Herman Donkers' identity card and punishment record.

CHAPTER 10 TAKEN TO THE CLEANERS

SEVEN MONTHS after his failure to escape with Hyde-Thompson, Herman Donkers was summoned by Capt. Machiel van den Heuvel, the Dutch Escape Officer. He wanted to know if Donkers was ready to take part in a plan more perilous than his previous attempt. Donkers could barely contain his enthusiasm and readily accepted the invitation.

Van den Heuvel added that the attempt would involve two more of his countrymen, Lt. Cdr. Damiaan van Doorninck and Lt. Ted Beets, and three British officers, Capt. William 'Lulu' Lawton, of the Duke of Wellington's Own Regiment, Hank Wardle, and Flt. Lt. Bill Fowler of the RAF. If they were successful in getting out of the Castle, Donkers would pair off with Wardle, van Doorninck with Fowler and Beets with Lawton.

The plan, like so many escapes, came about through the observation of the routine necessary to maintain an efficient structure of existence within a stronghold such as Colditz Castle.

On this occasion, it had been observed that the weekly task of four Polish orderlies offered an ideal escape route out of the Castle. The chore was the collection of dirty German uniforms and underclothing from a store room adjoining the outside of the Castle's north-facing wall. The orderlies, after loading the clothing into two large wooden boxes, were escorted under guard through a security gate to a building, known as the Zschadrass, a quarter of a mile from the Castle, where they washed and ironed the clothes.

The route provided excellent access to the Castle park. The plan, therefore, was to impersonate the orderlies and the two guards. It would take place in broad daylight and require a high degree of nerve as the bogus guards, without a special security disc pass, would have to bluff their way past the sentries. There was also the problem of how to get into the store room on the outside of the Castle wall.

Pat Reid discovered it was situated below the office of a Regimental Sergeant Major named Gephard. The floor of the office, Reid noticed, was at a slightly lower level than the roof of the store room on the other side of the wall. By removing the floorboards, he considered it possible to burrow through the wall, at a point beneath a window where the wall was no more than eighteen inches thick, and drop through into the store room.

The next problem of how a team could work undisturbed in Gephard's office was removed by the convenient location of the prisoners' sick ward just across the corridor.

It was agreed that a two-man team would hide under the beds and begin work after the main ward doors had been locked for the night. The ward doors and the doors to Gephard's office would be unlocked by Kenneth Lockwood, a Captain of the Queen's Royal Regiment, who was to get himself hospitalised by feigning a stomach disorder. He would also ensure that the doors were locked after the night's work was done with the duplicate keys supplied by master locksmith van Doorninck.

At the request of the British Escape Officer, Dick Howe, Pat Reid agreed to undertake the task of breaking through from Gephard's office to the store room. He was to be assisted by Lt. Derek Gill, of the Royal Norfolk Regiment. The supplying and fitting of two German uniforms and Polish orderly clothing were already under way. Van Doorninck would play the part of a sergeant with Donkers as a private. Donkers, an expert forger, used his talents to make the necessary identity papers for the 'officers' and the work permits and other documentation for their later roles as Dutch civilian workers.

It was now late August 1942. Lockwood, successfully feigning illness, had got himself safely tucked up in the sick ward and was ready for a visit

The Castle sick ward. It was from here that the escape began.

from Reid and Gill. They arrived to extend their sympathies to their sick colleague – and then, when all was clear, disappeared under the beds of collaborating patients. Some minutes later the ward was locked for the night. On a signal from Lockwood, they reappeared. The lock of Gephard's office door was a mere formality. Lockwood locked his colleagues in and returned to the ward.

Inside Gephard's office, Reid and Gill quickly removed floorboards near the outside wall and took turns at scraping away at the old mortar between the granite blocks. Over the years it had deteriorated badly and now offered little resistance. They worked through the night and by the first light of dawn had exposed the facing plaster of the wall inside the store room. Enough had been achieved. It had been a good night's work.

Blankets and sacking were placed in the hole to prevent it amplifying any sound caused by the footsteps of Gephard and his soldiers. Reid and Gill paid great attention to ensuring that everything was as they had found it, even down to the floorboard nails, while the gaps between the floorboards were carefully filled with dust collected earlier from the British quarters.

They were ready when Lockwood unlocked Gephard's door at a pre-arranged time and resumed their positions under the beds of their colleagues, slipping out of the ward at the appropriate moment and returning to their quarters in time for morning roll call.

The next night, Reid and Gill returned to widen the hole to take a man, still making sure the plaster on the other side of the wall was left intact.

It was agreed the attempt would be made reasonably soon after a collection by the Polish orderlies. That way, it was logically reasoned, there was considerably less chance of the escaping British and Dutch officers bumping fatally into a genuine expedition.

The date was uncertain because the orderlies' visits to the store room varied but were rarely more than twice a week. The best time of day would be shortly after 7 a.m. when the guards at the security gate were relieved. Howe and his colleagues were confident that the guards coming on duty would simply suppose that the laundry detail had entered

the store room before their guard duty had begun.

Everything was ready: the uniforms, orderlies' clothes, civilian clothes, the forged documentation – and the all-important wooden laundry boxes, complete with rope handles, looking identical to the real articles.

The wooden boxes were smuggled in sections into the ward by visitors and hidden under beds. They were followed by the British and Dutch team – Lawton, Fowler, Wardle, van Doorninck, Beets and Donkers – who arrived at varying times after the final roll call, as did Reid and Gill.

The drop into the store room was planned for 2 a.m. the following morning. They were allowing three hours for the completion of the operation. It gave the men plenty of time to climb through the hole, pass through their escape gear and make good the hole on the other side, for which Gill had brought with him an illicitly acquired bag of plaster and a container of water.

Shortly before 10 p.m. they settled down to wait in Gephard's office. It was too early to go forward and, if the Germans carried out one of their frequent spot searches, it was too late to go back. They had reached the point of no return. It was just before midnight when the sense of frustrating in-

Above: The store room running along the chapel wall, on the north side of the Castle. This fabricated building originally had its entrance in the tower at the north-west corner of the prisoners' yard, but this door was walled up after POWs were discovered tunnelling there. Another entrance was made on the outside wall and it was by this route that the escapers left.
Right: Ted Beets, Royal Netherlands Indies Army.

activity was instantly obliterated by one of total fear. The night noises of the Castle were wiped out by the piercing stridency of a security alarm.

There was nothing the men could do, but remain absolutely still. To try to get back into the ward would have been disastrous. Their worst fears were soon confirmed. A German patrol was searching that very part of the Castle. They could hear the stamp of approaching German boots, then every word of the orders being issued by a senior officer to soldiers standing just a few feet away, on the other side of the door of Gephard's office.

Only a few minutes earlier, they had been revelling in thoughts of a life free of Colditz Castle. Now they were waiting to be ordered to their feet at the point of a gun barrel. They heard the officer bark out an instruction to the soldiers. They couldn't believe their ears. '*Diese Tür ist gut verschlossen. Sie*

ist sicher. Lass es schon!' he told them. (This door is well padlocked. It is safe. Do not bother.) The soldiers moved on. It was some minutes before anyone dared to speak. They couldn't believe their incredible luck. After that incident, Donkers felt strangely elated. Nothing else, he thought, could happen that night that would bring them so close to capture.

The night passed on until, at the stroke of two o'clock, Reid and Gill stirred and began to lever gently at the floorboards. The blankets and sacking were removed from the hole, and, as carefully and noiselessly as possible, Reid pushed through the plaster separating them from the store room.

Van Doorninck was the first to wriggle, feet first, through the angled hole to drop safely into the store room. He was followed by Lawton and the others. Reid, who would remain behind with Gill to replace the floorboards, passed through the sections of the wooden boxes and the bogus German uniforms and other clothing.

The wooden boxes were quickly assembled. Van Doorninck put on his sergeant's uniform,

Below: A group of Polish orderlies at Zschadrass.

Donkers his private's, and the other four men transformed themselves into Polish orderlies. Van Doorninck began plastering over the hole in the wall. On the other side, Reid and Gill had already replaced the floorboards and made a successful exit from Gephard's office.

By ten minutes past seven the escape party was ready to leave the store room. Lawton, Fowler, Wardle and Beets grabbed the rope handles of the boxes. Van Doorninck opened the store room door and led them out into the cold, biting morning air, with 'Private' Donkers bringing up the rear.

Feldwebel Gebhard, nicknamed Mussolini, was in charge of the orderlies. He was killed in Russia 1944. Above: The hole leading from Feldwebel Gebhard's office to the store room below. Above right: Corp. Schaedlich, assistant to Feldwebel Gebhard, had a sharp eye for anything out of the ordinary and a keen nose for tunnels. The British nicknamed him Dixon Hawke and the French 'la Fouine' (the ferret). He owned the Hotel Wettiner Hof in Colditz town and was later killed in the Italian campaign.

The Germans were able to reconstruct the escape, using genuine Polish orderlies, and so acquired another picture for their museum.

The six men walked confidently past the first sentry, who paid them no attention. The second, some fifty yards on, barely gave them a glance either. The real test would come at the security gate. Van Doorninck did not have a key to the gate. He couldn't risk fumbling around with his lock-picking tools. He would have to order the sentry to open the gate.

But the sentry proved an unwitting ally. He didn't have to be ordered to open the gate. He asked van Doorninck: *'Gehen Sie zum Zschadrass?'* (Are you going to the Zschadrass?) Van Doorninck gave a curt affirmative reply, and the sentry obligingly unlocked the gate. The eight men marched through. They had pulled it off. They continued walking down the sloping pathway. They walked along the rear of the married quarters and ducked into a wooded area of the park known as the Tiergarten.

Donkers paired off with Wardle, van Doorninck with Fowler, and Beets with Lawton. They were soon over the stone wall – and fleeing through the countryside on their separate routes to Switzerland.

The German Security Officers were staggered when morning roll call was held and they discovered that ten prisoners were missing. The British and Dutch had decided to make use of the escape to hide four more officers as a cunning ruse for more escapes. If the Germans failed to find the hidden officers, they would assume they had escaped and the 'ghosts' could be kept in hiding until it was their turn.

As for the genuine escapers, Lawton and Beets were recaptured later that evening. Donkers and Wardle fared little better, being spotted next day while waiting for a train at a railway station some distance from Colditz. However, van Doorninck and Fowler were successful. They finally crossed the Swiss border on 15 September, 1942 – just six days after taking the escape-proof Castle's security system to the cleaners.

September, 1942. The first Navy types to arrive at Colditz.
Front row, left to right: Lt. Ernie Champion, RNR; Lt.
Cdr. O. S. Stephenson, RN; (Bosun) John Crisp, RN;
Sub. Lt. Norman Miller, RNVR;
Back row, left to right: Lt. Hugh Bruce, RM; Lt. Jack
Keats, RNVR; Lt. Mike Moran, RNR; Lt. Mike Harvey,
RN; Lt. Bob Barnes, RANR; Lt. Trevor Beet, RN; Sub.
Lt. John Hoggard, RNR.
    All these naval officers, with the exception of Lt. Cdr.
Stephenson and Lt. Beet, had been together at Stalag XB,
Marlag.

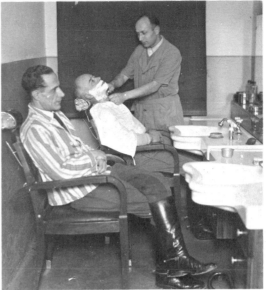

Left: Volley ball in the prisoners' courtyard. Above: Colditz International Sports Meeting scoreboard. Top: In the prisoners' barber shop. Above: The British corner of the courtyard.

THE MURDER OF SEVEN COMMANDOS

SEVEN COMMANDOS – one Canadian and six British – were temporary prisoners in Colditz Castle in October 1942 while en route for Berlin where, six days later, in flagrant violation of the Geneva Convention protecting prisoners-of-war, they were secretly executed.

They were captured shortly after carrying out a successful sabotage operation on a massive hydro-electric power station in occupied Norway. The mission, code-named 'Musketoon', was completed on 21 September, l942, by twelve commandos of the No. 2 Special Service Commando Unit. Only four escaped. They were Sgt. Richard O'Brien, of the Royal Berkshire Regiment; Cpl. John Fairclough, of the Grenadier Guards; Pte. Fred Trigg, of the Royal Sussex Regiment; and Cpl. Sverre Granlund, of the Royal Norwegian Army. Cpl. Høgwold Djupdraet, also of the Royal Norwegian Army, received a mortal bayonet wound while fleeing the devastated hydro-electric power station.

The seven commandos arrived in Colditz on 7 October, and their presence left the Kommandant, Oberst Glaesche, far from pleased. He had received no advance notice of their arrival, which was contrary to standing orders. However, he subsequently received orders from the Oberkommando der Wehrmacht to put the commandos in isolated custody until further notice. The following morning, all seven men were photographed by the official photographer, Johannes Lange. They were: Capt. Graeme Black (33), a Canadian serving with the South Lancashire Regiment, who led the mission; Capt. Joseph Houghton (31), of the Queen's Own

Cameron Highlanders, his second-in-command; C.S.M. Miller Smith (27), of the Coldstream Guards; L. Sgt. William Chudley (20), of the Royal Artillery; Pte. Reginald Makeham (28), of the London Scottish Regiment; Rfn. Cyril Abram (20), of the Rifle Brigade; and Pte. Eric Curtis (21), of the Queen's Own Royal West Kent Regiment.

Their arrival at Colditz marked their sixteenth day as prisoners, but they seemed to be under no illusion as to their fate. The NCO in charge of them was 'Tiger' Teicher, and perhaps the sight of this somewhat decrepit warrior, coupled with the fact they had no way of knowing they were being held in the most heavily guarded prison in Europe, prompted them to attempt an abortive escape that very night. A few days later Black and Houghton were transferred to prison cells in the town where Peter Storie-Pugh was already in solitary confinement for one of his many misdemeanours. Through the cell wall he was able to ask Black why they had been sent to Colditz. The leader of the commando team replied that he didn't know. But they had already been told, he added, that they were to be shot. Storie-Pugh, incredulous, refused to believe it, claiming that as they had been captured in uniform, their captors couldn't possibly do that.

The British contingent in the Castle was greatly concerned about the fate of their comrades. An official request by the Senior British Officer, Lt. Col. D. S. Stayner, to talk to the commandos was refused. The secrecy surrounding their arrival and the manner in which they were being kept in strict isolation gave credibility to Black's claim that they

From left to right: Capt. Joseph Houghton, Capt. Graeme Black, MC, Sgt. William Chudley, Pte. Reginald Makeham, Rfn. Cyril Abram, CSM Miller Smith, Pte. Eric Curtis. The loop-and-toggle ropes shown in some of the photographs were six feet in length and used, when inter-looped, for mountain climbing purposes. The commandos' shoes were particularly included in the photographs because they were a new design, considered at the time to be particularly effective for rock climbing. The heels also contained a compass, benzedrine tablets and a silk handkerchief which, when wet, revealed a map of the area of the hydro-electric station at Glomfjord.

were to be shot.

Their names were passed through illicit channels to London. The neutral Swiss authorities, among whose functions it was to represent the interests and welfare of prisoners-of-war, were notified and urged to intervene, but time was against them.

On Tuesday, 13 October, four SS officers arrived at Colditz. Black, Houghton, Chudley and Curtis were escorted out of the Castle under heavy armed guard. Abram, Makeham and Smith, similarly escorted, followed a short while later. They were all taken by the SS to Berlin for interrogation under the direct supervision of SS Obergruppenfuehrer Heinrich Mueller, superior officer to the notorious Adolf Eichmann.

Their successful Norwegian raid had set the German war effort back considerably and invoked the fury of Hitler. As a direct result of the raid, he issued a top secret order stating that in future all captured enemy commandos would be summarily executed.

It read:

From now on all enemies on commando missions, even if they are in uniform, armed or unarmed, in battle or in flight, are to be slaughtered to the last man. If it should become necessary to spare one man or two, for interrogation, then they are to be shot immediately after this is completed. In case of noncompliance with this order, I shall bring to trial before a court martial any commander or other officer who has failed to carry out his duty in instructing troops about this order or who has acted contrary to it.

The commandos were transferred on 22 October to a civilian concentration camp on the outskirts of Berlin called Camp Sachsenhausen. Shortly before dawn on 23 October they were each killed by a single shot in the back of the neck. Their bodies were conveniently disposed of in the camp crematorium. Of the four commandos who survived that mission, only Sgt. Richard O'Brien and Cpl. John Fairclough survived the war. Fairclough took part in four commando missions, was awarded the Military Medal and was demobbed in November 1945.

HOW THE FIXER FIXED A KISS

CHAPTER 12

THE CZECH RAF FLIGHT LIEUTENANT, Cenek Chalupka, had the talents of a master confidence trickster. He possessed a quicksilver mind, a glib tongue, the cunning of a freeloading fox and the engaging personality of a fund-raising evangelist. He was also without scruple when it came to exploiting the greed and weaknesses of any German soldier willing to smuggle into the castle materials for escape projects.

Chalupka, nicknamed 'Checko', was proud to be known as the Fixer, the Castle's black market baron who not so much enjoyed as revelled in his peerless reputation as the man who could obtain the unobtainable. His boast was that if it could be hidden under a German soldier's great coat, then he could acquire it. Much of the material required for the forging of work permits, passes and travel papers came through the hands of Checko, and his assistance, for example, in obtaining vital glue for the construction of the British prisoners' glider was of the utmost importance (see Chapter 18)).

But perhaps his most outrageous coup was one that had nothing to do with any escape attempt. It was motivated by romance. The focus of his lusty attentions was an attractive assistant who worked for the town's dentist. Checko was entranced by the young blonde woman after being taken to have an abscess treated. Certainly she did more for Checko than the dentist apparently could. In spite of his efforts, the abscess failed to respond to treatment. In fact, according to Checko's colleagues, it became unaccountably infected, which meant that his visits happily continued. However, the dentist finally became suspicious of the young man who seemed more interested in his assistant than the successful treatment of a painful abscess. Word was got to the Chief Security Officer and, in the interests of security, the young lady was to be transferred.

News of her impending departure somehow got to Checko's ears. There was certainly no way he could prevent it, but he did have enough corrupt sway to say a last farewell in romantic style.

A few days later Checko was to be observed standing impatiently by the trellis gate entrance to the prisoners' courtyard. Several British officers wondered what he was up to. Perhaps he was setting up a bribe? They remained at a discreet distance. A few moments later two soldiers appeared on the other side of the gate. They had with them a strictly unofficial visitor, the young dental assistant. Checko and the young woman stood as close to each other as the gate would permit. They said a few words and they kissed through the bars. She turned and walked away, flanked by the soldiers, and disappeared out of the Castle. They never met again.

Checko later revealed that he had paid a considerable bribe for the pleasure of the final farewell. It would, indeed, have had to be considerable to get her past the various security check-points. But it illustrated his remarkable ability to fix anything. Tragically, Flt. Lt. Chalupka died in an air crash soon after the end of the war.

A NIGHT ON THE TILES

IF EVER A MAN DESERVED to escape from Colditz Castle it was Lt. Peter Storie-Pugh. The slightly built, red-haired officer of the Queen's Own Royal Kent Regiment was captured in May 1940, when German infantry stormed the French village of Doullens, and was taken to Colditz that October. Like the vast majority of British prisoners-of-war he was destined to remain there until American forces swept through the town in April 1945. In that time he was involved in no less than twenty-one escape attempts, convinced that only in planning escapes,

however hopeless, could he survive the psychological stress of Colditz. The will to survive was all that mattered.

He was involved in one abortive British tunnel escape not many months after his arrival (see Chapter 1). In July 1942 his quick wits prevented the loss of valuable escape tools after another tunnel attempt, this time with the Dutch. Abandoning the subterranean, Storie-Pugh was later one of two British officers invited to join a remarkably daring rooftop escape devised by the Poles. The stateless Poles were in a perpetual condition of poverty compared with the British, who could sell surplus food to accumulate escape fund money. So Storie-Pugh and Capt. Cyril Lewthwaite bought their place in the escape attempt in return for a handsome cash contribution.

The Polish plan was to get out on the roof of a prison block in the inner courtyard at a point where it was only twenty feet from the roof of the Kommandantur, which gave access to the outer wall and the Castle park. They planned to throw a rope ladder across the gap and had even devised a bogus extra chimney stack as a piece of cover for the man fixing the ladder sixty feet above the ground.

The escape was foiled, however, by what had at first appeared to be one of its great assets – a night of driving rain and high wind which would surely have dimmed visibility and kept the sentries' heads down. On that particular night the wind was so violent that it caused a large shaded arc light suspended between the two buildings to swing so wildly that a Polish officer crawling across the ladder was caught for a split second in its arc of light at the precise moment when a soldier returning from town was attracted by the swaying lamp.

Because of his intense preoccupation with all matters of subversion, Storie-Pugh developed a secret code which he used in letters to his father. They began as early as June 1940, before he arrived at Colditz, and the key was his house at his old public school, Malvern. It was properly known as Hooper House, but always referred to as Number 9. In one of his letters Storie-Pugh inexplicably wrote: 'The number of letters from Hooper House show all one wants to know.'

At first the meaningless information puzzled his father. The rest of the letter was equally baffling,

The Polish contingent leave Colditz on their way to Spitzberg in Silesia, August 1943.

99

with no relevance to matters or people known to him, until he suddenly realised the significance of Hooper House – and Number 9. When he counted nine letters from Hooper House the words made no sense at all, but when he counted nine words he had the code. Storie-Pugh used this code right through until his release at the end of the war.

British intelligence supplied certain prisoners with codes of greater complexity, which were successfully used to transmit information from recaptured escapers that might be of possible intelligence value, such as sitings of munition supply dumps, troop movements or airfields.

Storie-Pugh senior also spared no effort in assisting his son to escape. He even decided to pursue a romantic tale he had heard about a touching love affair between a Countess, who had allegedly lived in Colditz Castle, and a handsome young townsman. According to the story, she got out of the Castle for their clandestine meetings through a secret passage.

He read every book he could possibly obtain

British quarters, July 1942. Front row, left to right: Lt. Jimmy Yule, RCS; Lt. John Watton, Border Regiment; Capt. Harry Elliott; Flt. Lt. Dominic Bruce; Lt. Grismond Davies-Scourfield, 60th, Rifles (KRRC); Capt. (Rev.) Richard Heard; Lt. Ralph Holroyd, Australian Imperial Forces; Lt. Kenneth Lee, RCS. Second row, left to right: Capt. Jim Rogers, RE; Capt. W. T. Lawton, Duke of Wellington Regiment; Capt. Pemberton-How, RASC; an orderly; Lt. Scorgie Price, Gordon Highlanders; Lt. John Davies, RN(A); Lt. Peter Storie-Pugh; Lt. John Boustead, Seaforth Highlanders; Lt. Bobby Colt, Tyneside Scottish Regiment; Lt. John Lace, Durham Light Infantry. Third row, left to right: Lt. Mike Sinclair; Capt. (Rev.) Ellison Platt; Lt. Geoffrey Ransome, NAAFI; Flt. Lt. Jack Zafouk; Flt. Lt. Peter Tunstall.
    This picture was taken within an hour of Lt. Storie-Pugh being found in the tunnel with Kruimink and van den Heuvel.
Bottom right: 1980, Col. Peter Storie-Pugh, MBE, MC, TD, DL, with a memento of his Colditz days, a map supplied by British Intelligence showing escape routes.
Right: The docket an officer received when he

did time in the punishment cells. One of many received by Lt. Peter Storie-Pugh requests that he presents himself in the prisoners' yard at 14.00 hrs to begin five days' cell arrest. He is allowed to bring with him bed linen, books, cigarettes or tobacco and toilet articles, but no food. His pay would be stopped for every day spent in the cells.

Colditz, am 18.11.41

Herrn
    Leutnant Stoire P u g h, bitte am 18.11.
41, um 14 Uhr im Hof zum Strafantritt einzu-
treffen. (5 Tage) Bitte ausser Bettwäsche
Bücher und Rauchwaren, Toilletenartikel keine
Lebensmittel mitzunehmen.

100

about historic and medieval German castles, but none made any reference to the passage, much less the countess. In desperation, he wrote to a museum librarian requesting assistance. He said he was making the inquiry on behalf of his son, an army officer. He didn't mention that he also happened to be a prisoner-of-war in Colditz Castle.

Back came the reply:

I have your letter of the 11th inst. I'm sorry I can't give you much information about the Castle Colditz. The present building was erected in 1464. I don't know anything about this story of the countess nor of the passage. If your son is allowed to send letters to people in Germany, I suggest he should write to Herren Dr. Boder Ebhart Marksfeld of Braubechen Rhein. He is the greatest authority on German castles. I'm quite sure he will do everything to help him.

Storie-Pugh Junior didn't bother.

An Anglo-Dutch operation, 26 July, 1942. Capt. van den Heuvel, Lts. Kruimink and Storie-Pugh exiting from a hole in their mess-room wall – an entrance to a tunnel that led to a disused attic in the Kommandantur.

Realising the game was up, Storie-Pugh, ignoring the shouts of the armed guards to 'Raus, Hände hoch! Schnell! Schnell!' delayed stepping down from the passage entrance until sufficient POWs, all eager to help, had crowded into the room. Wide-eyed and feigning complete astonishment at the size of Colditz 'Mouseholes', they hemmed in the guards, making any movement by them virtually impossible.

In the mêlée, Storie-Pugh was able to grab hold of a bag containing their much-valued escape tools and fling it over the Germans' heads. Wtihin minutes it was spirited away to a place of safety. Left to right, Lt. Frits Kruimink, Capt. van den Heuvel, Lt. Peter Storie-Pugh.

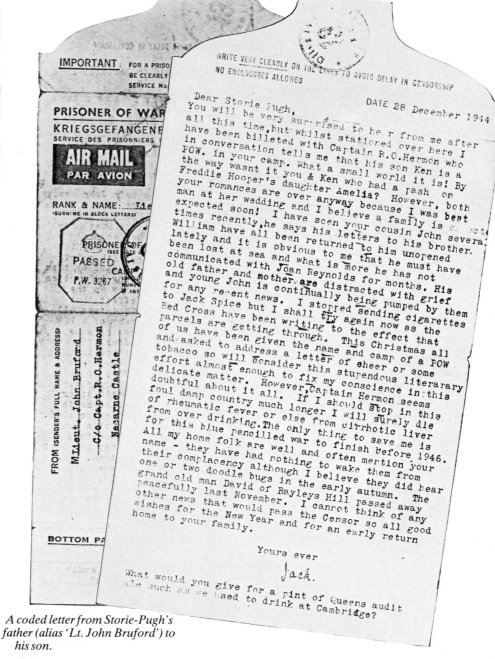

A coded letter from Storie-Pugh's father (alias 'Lt. John Bruford') to his son.

STEAL- AND BE DAMNED

WHEN IT CAME to acquiring materials for possible escape projects the first rule was: if it can be stolen, steal it. Efforts to divert the attention of guards, visiting officials and Castle maintenance workers in pursuance of this philosophy were remarkable in their mischievous audacity.

The prisoners' reputation was so feared that some members of the local citizenry in the town of Colditz, such as the dentist who on one occasion had his coat stolen, simply refused point-blank to visit the Castle to treat prisoners-of-war.

One classic example involved a building worker who, ordered to carry out repair work to an outside wall in the prisoners' courtyard, was craftily diverted in conversation long enough for his ladder, resting against the wall, to be whipped away, a length sawn off and the rest returned to its original position. Such thievery, apart from providing escape material, was equally important as a morale-raising sport to break the monotony of life in Colditz Castle, as was pointing out to the Kommandant that his English was not absolutely correct on the park perimeter wire notice which stated that prisoners attempting to escape in going beyond the wire would be shot. Now that, some of the prisoners mischievously reasoned, just couldn't be right. If a prisoner-of-war attempted to escape by climbing over the fencing, it didn't *necessarily* mean that he would be shot. After all, he might succeed and manage to get safely away. No, clearly what the Kommandant meant was that he would be shot at. The Kommandant, one cannot say how begrudgingly, conceded the point. The notices were duly corrected.

Willy Pöhnert featured as the unfortunate victim in one of the most successful bits of thievery, though it threatened to land the affable little electrician in a lot of trouble, particularly as it happened shortly after the Perodeau affair.

Willy was fixing a light in the ceiling of the prisoners' theatre. Because his bag of tools represented valuable booty, a soldier stuck to Willy like his own shadow. The bag, which, against all the rules, also contained Willy's pass keys to the Castle's many rooms, was at all times to stay within arm's length of the soldier.

It presented an irresistible if formidable challenge to the British who happened to be rehearsing a variety show in the theatre at the time. Their antics certainly amused the soldier, who was standing near the tall ladder which reached up to the theatre's high ceiling. At the top of the ladder was Willy, all too busy on the installation to give any attention to the British prisoners-of-war below.

They came closer and closer with their high-kicking dance routine, the soldier totally absorbed by the sight of big, hairy-chested men acting like Tiller girls – until Willy climbed down the ladder and inquired after the whereabouts of his bag of tools.

Nearly forty years later, at his home in Kurt Boehme Strasse, Colditz, Willy recounted the incident: 'The soldier had not realised it had gone – and he put it between his feet for safe keeping! Obviously, while he was paying so much attention to the British, one of them had crept up and removed it.

'There was a big panic. The soldier was so worried. He kept shouting at the prisoners, but they pretended not to understand. He kept demanding that my bag of tools be returned. They just looked at him with puzzled expressions on their faces and said nothing. The angrier he got and the louder he shouted, the more puzzled they pretended to be.

'I felt very sorry for him because I knew what terrible trouble he was in, but in a way it was funny. The British prisoners-of-war, dressed in their funny women's clothes, looked like angelic children, shrugging their shoulders at each other as if he was mad.

'One or two, trying to show they were concerned, spoke in German to him, and asked him what had happened and what was wrong. That made him much angrier. He kept repeating: '*Wo ist die Tasche*?' (Where is the bag?), but by then he realised he was wasting his time.

'He knew it was hopeless and that he would

have to report the matter. Before he walked away, he looked at me in such a pleading way, as if I could do something. There was nothing I could do. I was just a civilian and it had been his job to guard my bag. I didn't like him, anyway.'

A *Sonderappell*, a special roll call, was ordered and the six to seven hundred prisoners-of-war formed in ranks in the courtyard. A Senior German Officer, speaking directly to the British, ordered the return of Willy's bag. There was no response. He repeated the order. Again, it was met with total silence.

'Then the Senior Officer did something that was very clever,' said Willy. 'He summoned me to stand by his side in front of the men and request the return of my bag. It was clever because he had been told I got on well with the men and he knew they would not want to get me into trouble.

'As I stood in front of all these men, I felt so small. I said: "Please give my bag back to me." They said nothing. The Senior Officer said: "Please be so kind as to return Willy's bag." There was still silence. I did not know what to do. For a moment I believed they would not help me.

'The first time I spoke to them I said it in English. Because my English then was not good, the officer told me what to say. Then I became so nervous I pleaded with them in German.

'Suddenly, a voice from the back shouted: "Willy, you will have your tools back in two hours." I was so relieved I cannot describe it. I turned to the officer to see if he was pleased. His expression had not changed.

'We all just stood there. For the entire two hours. Then, exactly two hours later, there was a movement at the rear of the ranks of prisoners. I could see something was being passed towards the front. Finally, an officer in the front rank stepped forward with my bag and placed it in my hands.

'But I was still worried in case anything was missing. None of it was my fault, but the officers did not understand things like that. I could not bear to think about the keys. I was so happy when it was examined and it was all there.

'I suppose they did a copy of the keys. That is why we had to wait two hours. The Senior Officer probably realised that, although there was nothing he could do. The prisoners-of-war were not punished. Nor was I. I don't know what happened to the soldier, though.

'I felt very grateful to the British. They knew I was in serious trouble because when the Senior Officer made me ask for the return of the bag, he was putting the responsibility for its absence on me.'

Added Willy: 'I think the British knew that. To me, they were good men – and gentlemen.'

Willy Pöhnert and his coveted tool bag, with Slim, the carpenter.

July 1943. The Belgians arrive at Colditz station. Centre left: Capt. Hans Lange, Security Officer, talking to the camp Kommandant, Col. Schmidt. The short journey from station to castle was always a hazardous one for Security, and later they refused to accept responsibility for prisoners until they were safely inside the Castle walls.

Some of the first Belgians to arrive. Rear centre. Lt. Jan Scheere, an Olympic pentathlon athlete. He arrived at Colditz after beating up an informer who had betrayed the escape of two other Belgian officers at his former camp. His friends admiringly referred to him thereafter as 'the Belgian assassin'.

THE SECRET GHOSTS

A MINIMUM NUMBER of thirty officers had to be produced before permission was given for daily exercise in the park. Quite naturally, in times of cold or dull weather only the Spartan few would stand by the prisoners' yard gate, calling for their friends to join them and make up the required quota. On 5 April, 1943, a cold, blustery day, the guards were surprised and a little suspicious to find 150 fresh air fanatics all jostling each other in their eagerness to reach the park.

After the count was taken and some sort of order prevailed, they moved off towards the gate that would lead them out across the German yard. As they reached the arched gateway, a Dutch officer in the castle called down to them, 'All the Dutch officers come back, there is a lecture on.' Immediately the Dutch contingent about-faced and began to retrace their steps, colliding with other Allied officers, causing utter confusion amongst the ranks.

The guards' attempts to sort out the disorder only made matters worse, and soon the gateway was jammed with POWs, many of whom didn't know for certain, but guessed, that their Dutch friends were up to something.

On the other side of the archway, in the German yard, two German officers extricated themselves from what appeared to be an undisciplined rabble and quietly made their way to the gate across the yard and leading to the park.

The sentry on the gate demanded their passes and was satisfied to learn that they were officers of the Oberkommando der Wehrmacht, Berlin, on a visit to the Castle and their passes contained all the necessary stamps and signatures of both the Castle Kommandant and his adjutant. With identity established, the sentry saluted and moved to open the gate for Capt. Dufour of the Royal Netherlands Indies Army and Flt. Lt. van Rood, an RAF pilot of Dutch descent. The affable Dufour, perhaps overconfident, gave the guards a wave and a smile, a friendly gesture that caused their undoing, for a gold tooth at the front of Dufour's upper set was recognised by Guard Sgt. Grünert (nicknamed 'Nicht Wahr' by the British), who by the cruellest of luck just happened to arrive at the gate at the same time.

Their capture was followed immediately by the mandatory roll call, which established that two men were missing – Flt. Lt. Jack Best of the RAF and Lt. Michael Harvey of the Royal Navy. The authorities deduced that the escape plot had been an Anglo-Dutch affair, not an unreasonable conclusion given the close liaison that was known to exist between the two nationalities, and that the Britishers, preceding their colleagues, had successfully escaped.

Best and Harvey were never caught, which is hardly surprising considering they had not left the Castle in the first place. Their disappearance was a ruse pre-arranged to synchronise with the Dutch attempt, which enabled the British to extend considerably the scope of their escape activities. For the two Englishmen, from the moment of their disappearance, became ghosts and remained in hiding day and night. This meant they could work on escape projects without the interruption of daily roll calls. They could also play identical roles to the Dutch dummies and appeared in roll calls for a few days to cover for the absence of prisoners who had actually escaped. The risk of detection was slight. With six to seven hundred prisoners to count, a roll call was a laborious necessity. As long as the number tallied, all was well.

Best and Harvey were assigned by the British escape committee to work on a tunnel project. For as many as sixteen hours a day, seven days a week, and for week after week, they burrowed underground until they were at the point of exhaustion. They snatched their sleep during the day, sleeping in the beds of fellow officers, who continued the work as well as they were able between roll calls.

The tunnel was, however, a hit-or-miss affair, imprecise in its direction and eventual exit. Like the earlier French tunnel, it went under the floor of the prisoners' chapel and followed the direction of heating pipes which were believed to lead to the prisoners' kitchen and beyond to a boilerhouse in the German quarters. It was hoped to launch the escape from that area. However, such considerations were to prove academic. Two months after work had begun a German soldier discovered by chance a camouflaged trap door to the tunnel.

Fortunately, Best and Harvey were not in the tunnel at the time. They were still free to operate, although the continuous knife-edge tension of their run-and-hide existence was beginning to take its toll. Best, normally buoyant and optimistic, became introspective and morose. He would stand by the barred window of his quarters and look out on the tranquillity of the surrounding countryside, pressing his nose against a bar so that he could not see it, fantasising over the joy of freedom. But his days as a ghost were coming to an end, as was the year of 1943. He was soon to celebrate the New Year with a daring and hazardous escape plan that would finally get him out of Colditz Castle.

Capt. Dufour, left, and Flt. Lt. van Rood in borrowed plumage. Overleaf: The British contingent in Colditz, December 1942.

CHAPTER 16 IF ALLAH IS WILLING

Flt. Lt. Jack Best.

JACK BEST was an obvious choice to take part in the escape plan of Ulster-born Lt. Michael Sinclair, of the King's Royal Rifle Corps. Because the Germans believed he had successfully escaped some months earlier, they would hardly be searching for him in the event of a genuine escape, which greatly increased his chances of getting safely back to England.

He had also earned the right to make the attempt, for he had toiled ceaselessly and ungrudgingly on escape plans and the production of escape material for the benefit of others. Another factor in favour of his selection by the British escape committee was that he got on well with Sinclair, a lone and introspective character who did not make friends easily.

Sinclair was an irrepressible escaper, whose red hair, ingenuity and guile had earned him the nickname among the Germans of 'Der Rote Fuchs' – The Red Fox. Following his capture in the early days of the war, he made no less than eight escape attempts, sometimes almost reaching an Allied border before recapture.

Sinclair's latest plan was simple, but its success depended upon split-second timing. For at its heart was one vital minute when, Sinclair maintained, a weakness was exposed in the Castle's security routine.

He was supremely confident that it would work. He had to be. In that fleeting spasm of time, the two men would have to climb out of a window of the British quarters, drop thirty feet by rope to an upper terrace which was uncomfortably close to a rear door of the German soldiers' guard house, run about twelve yards across the terrace to a parapet over which they would descend some forty feet by rope to a garden area at ground level and then, after a frantic dash of about thirty yards across the garden, cut through barbed wire fencing which bordered the precipice, leading to the outskirts of the town. All in just sixty seconds and in what appeared to be impenetrable security conditions.

The window of the British quarters, from which Sinclair proposed the attempt should begin, was on the outer west-facing wall of the Castle. The area was, to put it mildly, well guarded. At the north-west corner of the British quarters building was a machine-gun tower, manned night and day, which gave a perfect view of the window, the upper terrace and the garden across which Best and Sinclair would have to run. There were also two manned machine-gun points situated in the garden area, one in the north-west corner and the other some 150 yards further along at the far end of the garden. They were positioned in front of the barbed wire fencing, beyond which was the steep drop of the precipice.

Jack Best in 1980.

Sinclair planned to cut through the barbed wire fencing at a point approximately equidistant from the machine-gun sentries.

What made his incredible plan feasible were the sixty seconds that elapsed between darkness descending and the Castle's powerful search lights being switched on. The delay was caused by instructions from Berlin to save electricity!

As darkness fell, it became increasingly difficult for the sentry in the machine-gun tower to see the west side of the Castle wall in detail. So it was the sentry's practice to join his colleagues in the garden area at ground level, until relieved by the night duty sentries, by which time the search lights were switched on. Sinclair maintained that under the cover of darkness there was sufficient time for his plan to stand a chance of success, and although it was an enormous gamble with many areas of potential disaster, the British Escape Officer, Dick Howe, gave it his approval.

To sharpen their agility, a wooden frame was constructed to the dimensions of the small second-floor window through which Sinclair and Best would begin their escape. Initially, their efforts were slow and clumsy, but as time and again they launched themselves through the mock window their movements became increasingly athletic until, finally, it was almost a matter of instinct.

It was agreed that Sinclair would go first through the window and down a ninety-feet length of bed-sheet rope. By the time Best had reached the halfway terrace, Sinclair would have thrown the end of the rope over the parapet and be on his way down to the garden area below. Best, once in the garden, would give a sharp tug on the rope as a signal for his colleagues to haul it back in. The two men would then face the most dangerous stage, the thirty-yard dash across the exposed garden to the barbed wire fencing. There, if they got that far, Best would attach a home-made grappling iron to a post for the fifty feet descent down the precipice while Sinclair tackled the barbed wire with a pair of wire cutters made for them by Flt. Lt. Bill Goldfinch, an active back-room escape worker.

The prisoners' orchestra rehearsed high above the British quarters and its conductor had a bird's eye view of the entire area. It was agreed the moment the night sentries arrived to relieve their colleagues, the orchestra would strike up a rousing piece of music. From that instant, Sinclair and Best would be on their own.

Once at the bottom of the precipice, they would skirt the town and make for a railway station beyond Colditz. Their destination was Holland, and the plan was to pose as Flemish workers on their way home after working in Germany. The choice of nationality was for Best's benefit, as his German, unlike Sinclair's, was non-existent and it was unlikely he'd be challenged in Flemish.

On the evening of 19 January, 1944, as darkness was descending on the British quarters, a crescendo of music launched Sinclair feet first through the window on his stomach, while Best came a split-second behind, head first on his back, adamant that it was easier and quicker for him that way. His feet scarcely touching the Castle wall, he was on the terrace within seconds.

Sinclair was already across the terrace, over the parapet, and halfway down the next section of the rope to the garden below. A moment later, Best was by his side. Sinclair, crouching low, ran the thirty yards across the garden, throwing himself to the ground when he reached the other side, and ready to cut through the barbed wire fencing with the cutters he had tied to his right leg.

As others see him   As

Best was about to make his move when he was stopped in his tracks by a sudden arc of light from the opened door of the guard house and a German soldier's voice coming from the terrace above. They didn't know it at the time, but in their descent one of them had brushed against a bell push to the guard house rear entrance on the terrace.

The soldier was standing only yards away from the rope which ran from the window and over the terrace parapet to Best in the garden below, and heard the sound of it whipping through the darkness as it was wound in. It was followed by another noise – the 'ping' of barbed wire being cut by Sinclair who, oblivious of the soldier's presence, was working to plan.

As the soldier returned to the guard house to raise the alarm, Best seized his chance to join Sinclair, who had now finished cutting through the barbed wire. They fixed a grappling iron to a post and dropped down the precipice, stumbling in the darkness, their clothes torn from cutting their way through rolls of barbed wire stretching across the precipice to reinforce security. A spike cut into Best's hand, but in the tension he felt no pain.

Sinclair also had a narrow escape. Ahead of Best, he suddenly disappeared down a ten feet deep quarry, lying there for several moments, stunned and shocked. Best believed he was unconscious. But without a word, Sinclair slowly got to his feet and carried on.

Then came another heart-stopping shock. As they neared the bottom of the precipice, they saw an old woman emerge from a house and walk into the garden which backed on to the precipice. They had no doubt that she saw them. She stood there for a few seconds, looking straight at them. Then, without a word, she turned around and went back into the house.

The two men, spurred on by the nervous excitement of what they had achieved, scrambled on down the last few feet of the precipice. They circled the old woman's house and made their way surreptitiously out of town. Once they were safely clear, they repaired the barbed wire tears to their clothes with a needle and cotton carried as an afterthought by Best.

The sense of elation experienced by Best was overpowering. He had been a prisoner-of-war for

An amusing sketch by Lt. John Watton portraying the thoughts of probably every escaping British officer on his route through occupied territory.

115

Left: Sinclair's false identity card, made out in the name of Oberfeldwebel Fritz Rothenberg, 'Franz Joseph'. The escapers didn't realise it at the time but the card was two days out of date. Right: The 'Red Fox' Lt. Michael Sinclair.

two years and eight months. Now he was free of Colditz Castle. He was convinced he would soon be back in England.

In the Castle the alarm had been raised and the prisoners were doing their co-operative best to delay the inevitable roll call, first by a well-aimed catapult at the main lamp in the courtyard, and then by fusing the lights altogether.

Meanwhile Sinclair and Best were making considerable progress on the night of their escape, assisted enormously by a Colditz-made compass, and by early morning they were within a couple of miles of a railway station. They were able to time their arrival at the booking hall to the last minute thanks to a rail timetable acquired through bribery at Colditz, and thereby minimised their exposure to the vigilant eyes of railway officials and police.

The first leg of their rail journey passed without incident. It ended at Sinclair's insistence at Naunhof, a small town just before Leipzig, because he felt it was far safer to cut across country and continue their journey from the next station down the line.

They also agreed to take only slow stopping trains. For it was well known, to the cost of more than one escaper, that express trains were more frequently boarded by security officials and police.

From Naunhof, Sinclair and Best began their trek across country, circuitously avoiding Leipzig, to reach the small town of Delitzsch by the morning of their second full day of freedom and here they

boarded a train to Bitterfeld, another small town a few miles away. At Bitterfeld they made their first mistake by boarding in error a train full of Polish labourers going to an armaments factory. Fortunately Sinclair, who had worked with Polish freedom fighters during one of his earlier escapes, struck up a conversation with one of the workers, and discovered they were heading away from their planned route to Holland. They took the risk of confiding their predicament to the man and he for his part helped them pick the right moment to jump from the train on to a wooded embankment. It took them three long hours to get back to Bitterfeld, and this time they made no mistake about getting on the right train which took them to Magdeburg, Braunschweig, Hanover, Osnabrück and on to Rheine.

By the morning of their fourth day on the run, they were desperately tired and hungry. Their meagre escape rations had gone and they were physically and mentally exhausted. Best wanted nothing more than to lie down and sleep for ever, but they had arrived at Rheine. Approximately sixteen miles away was the frontier town of Bentheim, and beyond that – freedom.

They planned to make their break into Holland

that night from an isolated point on the frontier a couple of miles south of Bentheim. Until then they had several hours to kill – and they were famished. Allowing their hunger to subdue their sense of caution, Sinclair bought a loaf of bread and some vegetable soup. It was a gastronomic feast.

They then agreed that the safest way of staying out of sight was in the local cinema where they could also snatch some sleep. But they arrived to find a heated row between some soldiers and the manager who was refusing them admission because the programme had already started. Sinclair and Best walked hurriedly past.

They were now at a loss for a place where they could unobtrusively while away the hours. If they had been less tired, or perhaps less complacent because they were so close to pulling off their escape, they would, believes Best, have opted for safety first and headed out of town until darkness fell.

Instead they stood in one of the town's main streets, mulling over their next move until their conversation was suddenly interrupted by the arrival of a police officer. They had paused to debate right outside the town police headquarters. Neither Sinclair nor Best gave a thought to making a run for it. They were too tired.

Inside the police station they were interrogated by several senior police officers. The atmosphere in the room, recalls Best, vibrated with hate. Best, pretending, as was indeed his case, to understanding little German, said nothing. Sinclair vainly attempted to maintain their stories about being Flemish workers returning to Holland. Best, instructed by word and exaggerated gesture to take off his overcoat, did so but saw Sinclair was keeping his on so he started to put his own back on. For this he was struck a vicious blow to the head, pushed to a corner of the room and spun round to face the wall. Even in his terrifying predicament, or possibly because of it, he couldn't restrain his reaction to the classroom-level punishment. He burst out laughing.

While the police officers continued to fire questions at Sinclair, Best deftly removed from an inside pocket two pieces of dog-eared Colditz lavatory paper on which he had mapped out directions to Bentheim. He screwed them up, slipped them into his mouth and swallowed them. But when their identity papers and documents were revealed as forgeries, both men realised their situation was hopeless.

It took only a phone call to the Oberkommando der Wehrmacht in Berlin to establish that two prisoners-of-war had escaped from Colditz and that Sinclair fitted the description of one of them. (Cleverly, when Best, the incumbent ghost, quit Colditz another prisoner, Lt. Barnes, took over the role and it was therefore Barnes who was reported missing with Sinclair.)

Once their status was established, Sinclair and Best were thrown into a cell. Its white-washed walls were spattered with blood. Two ragged mattresses

Lt. Alexander Lancelot Pope of the Royal Fusiliers impersonated a German sentry in the 'Franz Joseph' affair.

on the stone floor were also caked with blood. The cell had been used, Best believed, to torture Dutch men and women who had been caught working for the resistance. Despite the gory state of the mattresses, they presented the most inviting sight the two men had seen in days. Best gratefully collapsed on one. He was asleep almost instantly.

The next morning they were taken to a French prisoner-of-war camp to await collection for the return journey to Colditz Castle just eight days after they had left it.

On his return to the Castle, Best gave his name as Barnes. This had been pre-arranged in the event of his recapture to enable the real Barnes to continue ghosting.

Incredibly, Best's presence in Colditz Castle was concealed for eleven months and three weeks.

Officially, he had 'escaped' on 5 April, 1943, when he was hidden away with Lt. Michael Harvey following the unsuccessful Dutch escape attempt. It was only when Harvey himself was caught in an escape attempt with Australian Flt. Lt. 'Bush' Parker, that their identities were unravelled, in March 1944.

The Oberkommando der Wehrmacht was staggered when the full report reached them. They found it so incredible that a senior official was sent to investigate and it was originally thought that the two men had, in fact, escaped twelve months earlier but, being unable to get out of Germany, decided in desperation to break back in to the Castle!

Flt. Lt. Jack Best was not actively involved in any further escape break-outs. He finally left Colditz Castle for good on 15 April, 1945, when Combat Command R of the 9th Armoured Divison (Fifth Corps) of the U.S. First Army swept through Colditz on their way to link up with Allied forces.

Best, who became a farmer in Gloucestershire, said: 'Of all the things that could have gone wrong but didn't, it was astonishing that we should fail because a police officer happened to be looking out of his office window as we were standing a few yards away wondering where we could hide out until dark.

'It proved to me that no matter how brilliant the plan, how meticulous the preparations, how courageous the men, it would only work if Allah was willing.'

Sinclair made one more desperate attempt to escape, perhaps his most audacious yet, when he impersonated an elderly German Sergeant-Major whose immaculate and grandiose moustache had earned him the nickname Franz Joseph among the

prisoners. Sinclair, disguised as this World War One Iron Cross-winning worthy, and two other prisoners disguised as soldiers, were to relieve a guard post which would allow a column of no less than thirty-five officers to break out through a window.

The first sentry was dismissed without smelling a rat, the second began to follow, but turned back at the last minute and challenged the bogus Franz Joseph to show his pass. The game was up. It was a tiny detail which had been his undoing. The real Franz Joseph had always looked over both sides of the catwalk he was crossing when he relieved the sentries, and Sinclair, despite studying the old soldier's every mannerism, had failed to do so.

In the end it all became too much for Sinclair. He had made nine escape attempts with infinite care and forward planning and seen each fail, some when freedom was mere miles from his grasp. On a mild pleasant day in the autumn of 1944 he simply broke away from a group of his fellow officers ambling round the compound, hopped over a foot high wire which marked the three feet wide danger zone into which prisoners were forbidden to step, and threw himself at the wire.

He hauled himself up strand by strand, ignoring in his desperation the barbs tearing at his hands and clothing. It wasn't until he had reached the top that he was seen by a sentry and ordered to stop. But by then he had dropped to the ground and was running down the ravine towards the park wall. He was to get no farther. A volley of shots rang out. A bullet ricocheted off his elbow and pierced his heart.

At last he was free.

'Franz Joseph', centre.

119

INVITATION TO DINNER

IN THE CIRCUMSTANCES it could hardly be described as a black-tie affair, but the invitation for cocktails and dinner was, nevertheless, warmly accepted by several of the British officers. It came after all from their French colleagues who enjoyed a considerable reputation for their flair in creating appetizing meals from limited and mundane ingredients.

The evening indeed began with cocktails, albeit from the Frenchmen's crude still but nevertheless a potent brew that hinted favourably of the genuine product. They were followed by a three-course dinner, which the British, to a man, agreed was superb.

The main course prompted the most favourable comments. Garnished with a basic but tasty sauce, it had been the most succulent of rabbits. None had tasted better. There followed a toast by the French thanking the British for the pleasure of their company. The British responded by congratulating the French on the magnificence of the dinner. The French claimed, however, that the credit really belonged to the British. After all, had it not been a pet cat of one of the British officers that had so gallantly sacrificed itself under a French knife for the benefit of the diners?

On hearing of the French gastronomic evening, Lt. David Hamilton, of the 52nd Light Anti-Aircraft Regiment, Royal Artillery, became alarmed for his own pet cat and hid it in a long-disused oven in one of the Castle's kitchens. It proved, for the cat, a fatal move. As life's ironies dictate, the oven was called into service and the cat suffered premature cremation.

The Frenchmen's dinner table was not by any means the only occasion when cat meat was on the menu. Two Belgian officers, Lt. Louis Marlière and Commandant Flébus, were said to have been sent to Colditz for consuming a cat at a prisoner-of-war camp at Eichstätt. Perhaps their big mistake was consuming a German national.

Right: Commandant Flébus, the 'cat-eater', front row, second left. Above: Senior French officers, Gen. le Bleu and Col. Marc. They had arrived at Colditz in February 1941.

The order, issued by the camp Kommandant, reads: 'I punish the prisoner, Lt. Louis Marlière, No. 2984, with 14 days room arrest because he killed in a bestial fashion a German cat not belonging to him, cooked it, and together with Commandant Flébus devoured it in an unnatural manner, although the rations which are measured out to the prisoners are quite sufficient and excellently prepared.'

In respect of Flébus, the order read: 'I punish with 10 days arrest the prisoner, Commandant Flébus, No. 116, because he on the 2.3.41 captured a German cat not belonging to him and on the 4.3.41 took part in the unnatural consumption of the cat.'

Right: The prisoners' cookhouse. A group of French orderlies indulge in a little horseplay for the benefit of the photographer. Inset: An illicit still. The brewing societies of Oflag IV C managed to produce a number of potent-if-not-toxic brews from makeshift distilling plants hidden away in the dark recesses of the Castle. A little ingenuity coupled with Red Cross supplies of raisins, currants, dried figs or jam, sometimes a dash of eau-de-Cologne and yeast, bribed from a sentry, resulted in a vintage resembling TNT and the morning after many POWs were convinced it was.

THE FREEDOM FLIGHT

CHAPTER 18

Above: Lt. Michael Harvey, RN.

THERE HAS SURELY never been an escape plan from any prisoner-of-war camp as fantastic as that involving the Colditz glider. This home-made machine, with a wingspan of thirty-three feet, was a British brainchild and the officers involved in its creation were Flt. Lts. Bill Goldfinch and Jack Best, Lt. Tony Rolt of the Rifle Brigade, Capt. David Walker of the Black Watch and Lt. Geoff 'Stooge' Wardle, RN. Goldfinch, a professional draughtsman before the war, was responsible for its design; Rolt for organising and maintaining an elaborate and vital early-warning system; Walker for acquiring materials and Best, a versatile craftsman, for supervising its construction with Goldfinch.

It was built at one end of a long empty attic above the prisoners' chapel behind a false wall of plastered canvas-covered frames. The plaster was conveniently made from the French tunnel project debris and, once dried, it matched the surrounding walls perfectly and defied snap searches during the nine months of the glider's construction.

Another virtue of the attic was that it overlooked the roof of an adjoining building which could be used as a launching pad to catapult the glider clear of the Castle. On the day of the flight they would break through the attic wall, carry out the fuselage and the sixteen-feet wings, and assemble them on the roof on a trolley attached by a system of pulleys to a bathful of concrete. When dropped sixty feet through the Castle floors, Goldfinch calculated this should provide enough thrust to launch the two-seater glider along the sixty-feet ramp. He reckoned it would be launched at a speed of twenty-seven m.p.h. and could cover a distance of 900 feet.

The construction of the glider from the extra long floorboards of the theatre and blue and white check cotton sleeping bags turned into a massive British communal effort, but it was never put to the ultimate test. By the time it was finished in January

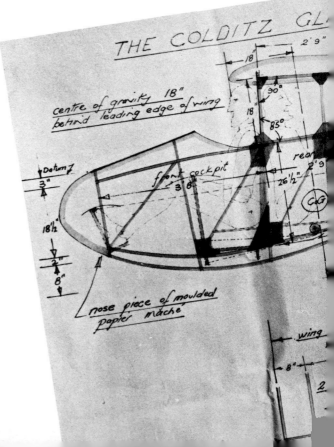

1945, the prisoners knew from broadcasts received on their secret wireless set that the end of the Second World War was in sight.

On 15 April a task force from the 9th Armoured Division of the United States First Army, sweeping in from the west to meet Allied armies at the centre of the Third Reich, stormed into the town of Colditz and liberated more than 300 British and Allied prisoners-of-war. That wondrous bird, a testimony to man's remarkable ingenuity in the most adverse of conditions and to his courageously stubborn refusal to accept defeat, was created never to soar in triumphant freedom from the captivity of Colditz Castle.

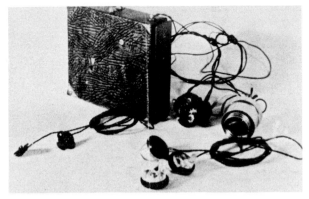

English radio containing miniature valves found under the floor in the Castle cellar 16 March, 1944.

The Colditz glider.

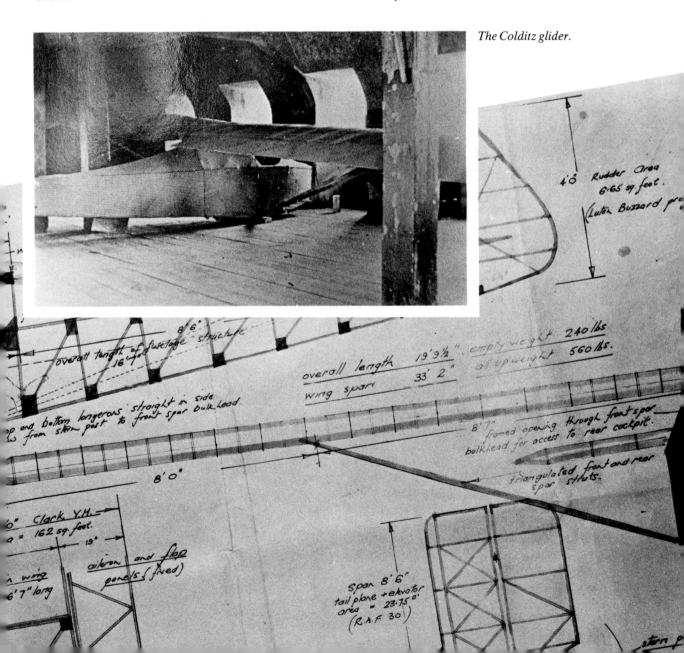

All the male population capable of using a weapon, young or old alike, had been conscripted into resistance groups in an attempt to stem the tide of the Russian advance only twenty miles to the east and the Americans in the west, virtually on the outskirts of the town. Food was non-existent, POW rations were down to a bare 1,300 calories a day. The roads by-passing Colditz were choked by hundreds of thousands of refugees, fleeing from the east, trusting they would get a better deal in the western-occupied areas.

Dresden and Leipzig just a few miles away were in ruins. Between 14–16 February, 1945, three heavy bombing raids by the British and Americans left an estimated 100,000–300,000 dead.

This picture shows refugees from farmsteads on the outskirts of Colditz town finding temporary sanctuary within the Castle walls. Their faces reflect the ravages of war. One wonders how the Nazi party member, a particularly healthy-looking specimen, managed to avoid the compulsory dragnet of conscription.

Below: 14 April, 1945. Safe conduct document given to Lt. Col. Prawitt, Kommandant of Colditz from May 1943, signed by the Senior British Officer, Col. Todd, Gen. Davies and Lt. Col. Duke.

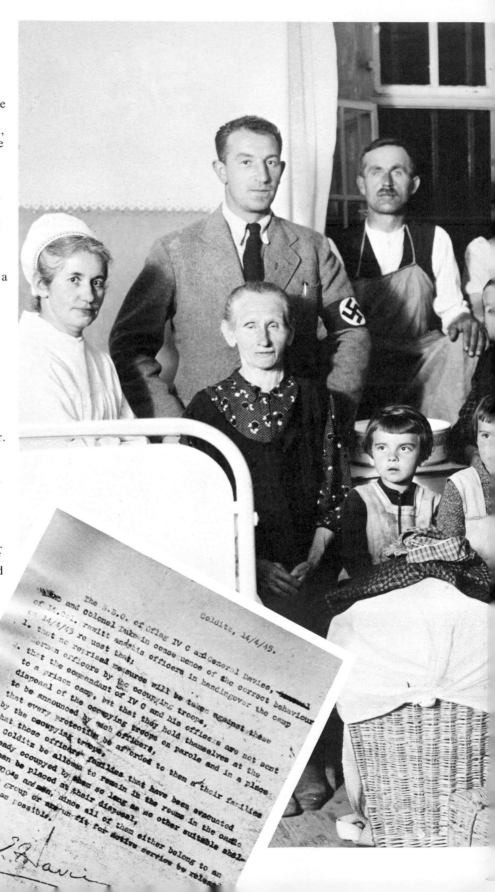

ACKNOWLEDGMENTS

I extend my grateful thanks to the many former inmates of Colditz whose generous help made this book possible. I searched the length and breadth of the United Kingdom and Europe to find the stories behind the faces and, having found them, they did not disappoint.

The biggest problem was to get people to tell their own story. They were only too willing to relate the escape of the chap in the Dutch or Polish quarters, or assure me, 'You should contact so and so. He's the chap to see, I have his address here somewhere.' However, with perseverance I was able to drag their own stories from them.

My heartfelt thanks to Lt. Cdr. Mike Moran (retired) for the invaluable information he was able to supply from his Colditz records. Mike Moran was the Colditz paymaster during the years this book deals with (when he wasn't engaged in escape activity, that is) and today he still continues his battle with Whitehall on behalf of ex-Colditzers, for money still owing them from their years of captivity.

I should also like to thank the following for their generous help in compiling this record: Col. Peter Storie-Pugh, MBE, MC, TD, DL (ret.); Jack Best, MBE; Capt. David K. Hamilton, ERD, (ret.); Dominic Bruce, MC, AFM, MA, FRSA; Col. Anthony P. T. Luteyn, (ret.); Col. Herman Donkers, MobK, (ret.); Lt. Col. Charles Linck, ROM, Bronze Star, KOV4, MobK, (ret.); Lt. Col. Dolf L. C. Dufour, DRF, (ret.); Col. Leo de Hartog, KOV4, MobK, (ret.); Col. Ted Beets, ON4 EOV 3 bars; Anthony T. Karpf; André Perodeau; and Willy Pöhnert.